SOUND
HEALING

Shirlie Roden

SOUND
HEALING

How to use the healing power
of the human voice

PIATKUS

© 1999 Shirlie Roden

First published in 1999 by
Judy Piatkus (Publishers) Ltd
5 Windmill Street
London W1P 1HF

The moral rights of the author have been asserted
A catalogue record for this book is available from the British Library

ISBN 0-7499-1989-2

Text design by Paul Saunders

Typeset by Action Publishing Technology Ltd, Gloucester
Printed and bound in Great Britain by
Biddles Ltd, Guildford

This book is dedicated with love and thanks to
Paul Solomon, Vesta Vanell, Suzannah Campbell
and my parents Joseph and Evelyn Roden,
not forgetting the Angels of Sound and the
many people who have inspired and supported me on my path.
Thank you for helping me understand who I am.

CONTENTS

Sounding Out Past Lives and Passed-over Relationships •
Empowering with Sound • Releasing Emotional Patterns
in Pairs • The HPA Axis • The Akashic Record • Sound
and Children • Passing Over Sounds

ACKNOWLEDGMENTS

Many thanks to: Soozi Holbeche for awakening the knowledge within me; John Christian for his inspiration and teaching; Angelica Roquas Hammer for her channelled readings from the Angels of Sound; Professor Janez Preželj at the Clinical Centre Ljubljana for his advice on endocrinology and medical matters; Tim Sikyea of the Dog Rib Tribe for his Native American wisdom; and Graham Wilson at New Life Promotions, Steve Heliczer at QED and Mark Rimminton at Bright Ideas for their continuing support in getting the knowledge out there.

FOREWORD

When I was asked to write the foreword for this book I immediately said 'Yes', because forward is where both Shirlie and myself are going. I consider myself privileged to know Shirlie and to have had the opportunity to conduct workshops together which we began to do in 1998 after a seven year friendship. She is the yin to my yang, and I the yang to her yin. During our lecture last year and the Festival of Mind Body and Spirit in London, I was a witness to her 'sound healing'. When she began, I must confess, I had fleeting doubts and thoughts of 'What am I doing here?' Seemed hippy trippy to me, and this rock and roller wanted to scream out in defiance. Well it took about 60 seconds for Shirlie's voice to pull me in, and I surrendered. If there is a truth that we all have a path to follow, then I am very pleased to say, Shirlie has found hers. She is a gifted healer but more importantly a genuine one.

To all who venture into these pages, read, enjoy and trust in Shirlie's abilities, she won't lead you astray . . . Rock on Shirlie . . . I'm with you in heart, soul and spirit.

Your friend and partner
Suzi Quatro

INTRODUCTION

This book has manifested itself expressly at the request of people attending my workshops, not the least my many friends and supporters in Slovenia, and is the sum of events which have served to open my intuition and completely transform the course of my life.

I was brought up in Wales – Land of Song and the Eisteddfod – with the proverbial opera singer living opposite, and sang and played the piano from an early age. My one ambition each year was to win the Girls' Vocal Solo in the High School Eisteddfod, and on a number of occasions I achieved it. My two elder brothers discovered rock and roll and formed rock groups, and the fateful day that Robin taught me to play a twelve bar blues Beethoven went out the window and Chuck Berry came dancing in.

When I was fifteen, my father bought me my own acoustic guitar and in the school holidays I ran away to London, intent on becoming a star. An earnest Joan Baez clone, I sang at Les Cousins and Bunjies coffee bar alongside emerging sixties' singer/songwriters like Al Stewart, Bert Jansch and the then unknown Paul Simon (who was kind enough to lend me his beautiful guitar on a couple of occasions). I even made it on to the cult television show *Ready Steady Go* in a Marianne Faithfull sing-alike competition.

Back home in Wales, piano gave way to singing lessons, and I learned diaphragm breathing which doubled the power and

range of my voice. I got a part-time job singing with a dance
band in a local night spot. Our bass player, Sid, was a lovely old
man from the valleys. 'There's something in your voice that
makes a man want to cry,' he often told me. I didn't understand
what he meant. All I knew was I had to sing, but I was now at a
musical crossroads. 'You can't study classical music and sing
that awful pop stuff,' my singing teacher remonstrated. 'You'll
ruin your voice.'

I made my decision. By 1971, when I graduated from university, I was signed to EMI Records with a group of fellow students
in the aptly named band Children. Ten years of working in rock
music followed. During this time my body was pounded with
throbbing bass tones, 200-watt high-pitched guitars and crash-
ing drums, not to mention voluminous quantities of alcohol
and the odd experimental excursion into illegal substances.

In 1977, while touring America with Ray Davies and the
Kinks, I underwent an extraordinary experience that transformed me and guitarist Dave Davies simultaneously. In
hindsight, I realize it was a 'spiritual awakening'. I felt a beam of
pure white light shining from the centre of my heart, which
linked me peacefully and lovingly to every living thing I came
into contact with. I intuitively and absolutely understood that
there was a divine plan of which we are all a part. So deeply was
I transformed into spirit that I perceived the body itself as
'clothing', and to put on clothes, let alone stage make-up,
seemed ridiculous.

For nearly two weeks Dave Davies and I vibrated at such a
high energy level that I could intuitively talk to and understand
plant life. Each night on stage he and I linked up: Dave stage left,
me stage right. The energy seemed to come from the back of my
head and crossed the stage in a vast arc of light to enter the back
of his head. It felt like a power grid on to which we drew down
light and then projected it into Ray as he performed. In our
altered states of consciousness, Dave and I instinctively knew the
importance of creating a good vibration from the band to send
out into the audience; and as we did our 'secret work' each night
the entire entourage, often fraught with arguments and bad
feeling, seemed to vibrate with harmony and peace.

As suddenly as it had begun the experience disappeared, bringing me back down to earth in Los Angeles. The real world had a strangely dull, monochrome look to it. Had it really happened? Maybe I'd dreamed it all? A newspaper review of one of our concerts seemed to say otherwise. It described an unaccustomedly small Kinks audience which Ray Davies just couldn't get going. That particular night, Dave and I had agreed to do our psychic 'link-up' at a certain song in the set. Amazingly, the reviewer reported:

> The turning point of the evening came with the first few strains of 'Lola'. Ray Davies seized control and bellowed 'SING!' Lo and behold, the crowd stood up as one. Even the band, energized by sparkling lead guitar work from brother Dave, seemed to burst at the seams. The tension eased from the air and Ray Davies began to glow a peace and contentment which seemed strangely antithetical to the blaring reverb and the theatrical rear projection light show.

But what on earth was it? Why had this strange energy suddenly come through me? And how would I discover it again?

It was another ten years before I found any kind of an answer to my questions. During that time, I worked extensively with my then partner and record producer, Jon Miller. With the incredible classic rock of the Gordon Giltrap Band I learned to use the high octaves of my voice as an instrument – not through any desire of my own, I might add, but because Gordon didn't want lyrics and Jon wanted his girlfriend in the band! At this moment I began to be aware of the energy of sound vibration, and that there was something in those high, pure notes which was both unusual and powerful. Then the Giltrap Band split up and I began to focus on a solo career as a singer/songwriter.

Dave Davies had phoned me a year after I had left the Kinks, on the anniversary of our spiritual awakening. 'Do you ever do anything to get back to that place?' he'd asked me. 'Like what?' I'd replied. 'Meditation,' he said simply. At university I'd been initiated into Transcendental Meditation during the Maharishi's first British outreach. Now, some years later, I decided to try TM again. Certainly I felt more peaceful and also seemed to get a lot of creative ideas during meditation.

It was now the punk era and there was no work for a melodic singer like me. Jon suggested I change direction and write a musical on the life of Joan of Arc, and *Jeanne* was born. Enter theatrical producer Bill Kenwright – not yet an impresario but an energetic optimist – who was impressed enough to say to film director John Boorman 'I've just heard something that's even better than *Evita*.'

Jeanne was a turning point in my life. Everything I had ever done up until the moment when it took the stage at Sadlers Wells had been for my own gratification, whether emotional, intellectual or material. I had wanted success, and I had wanted it for me. With *Jeanne*, to the best of my ability I had written the story of a young teenage girl whose visionary powers inspired her not only to lead the French army against the English, but later to stand alone in court with the entire might and knowledge of the Church ranged against her, and still to believe in her right to speak her own truth. It was a beginner's flawed piece of writing, but parts of it, I know to this day, were inspired. The critics tore the show apart and it closed prematurely.

Failure of any sort is difficult to handle, but failure in the public eye is particularly painful. My long relationship with Jon Miller was also floundering. Suddenly there was no work, no money and no future. I played endless games of patience and toyed with the idea of killing myself. How could I do it tidily, without upsetting friends and family?

But life had other ideas in store for me. Playing St Michael in my musical was an American, Chris Van Cleave. He and his wife Judith had been particularly kind to me as *Jeanne* closed, and invited me to join a weekly support group. They were part of something called The Fellowship of the Inner Light which they said was neither a cult nor a religious sect, but had been founded by an American teacher, Paul Solomon, who apparently believed that life was a Mystery School and that we ourselves create everything that happens to us as a challenge to grow and learn.

The idea that I had master-minded the incredible failure of

Jeanne and the end of my relationship with Jon specifically as part of my own growing process seemed ridiculous to me. But I needed to talk, so I joined the group and took the first step on a new path that began to open up in magical ways.

The first time I listened to one of Paul Solomon's lectures on tape, I was ironing in the kitchen and began to cry. He was talking about that place, that feeling, that light which Dave Davies and I had made contact with so long ago. In a rush of emotion I realized that other people too had experienced it. Paul called that power The Source and said we could all access it at any time.

I continued to study with Paul's tapes and with some of the teachers who had trained with him, notably John Christian and Soozi Holbeche. I learned the two most important lessons of my whole life: to take responsibility for my own emotions and feelings and in doing so to know that I always had a choice as to how I used my energy – negatively or positively. The reviews of *Jeanne* had so knocked my confidence, I had not sat at the piano for a year. Eventually I found the self-assurance to write music again, and this time it was different. They were songs of inspiration, of hope, of awareness.

Paul came to England to lecture a number of times during those years, and on one visit he and his entourage moved into my house. He let me sit in on his 'channelling' sessions where he accessed what is known as the Akashic Record to answer people's questions. It was simultaneously frightening and fascinating observing what American visionary writer Carlos Castaneda calls this 'separate reality'. Occasionally John Christian and I travelled with Paul to 'warm up' the audiences with songs before his lectures.

One night I sang for Paul in a village hall and a man approached me afterwards, telling me that when I sang he had seen me surrounded in white light, and that something had happened to him emotionally. A few weeks later, we met in London. Tony Benham was a potter and we found ourselves wandering around a glassblower's shop. On the floor in a corner was the most beautiful purple-blue glass object, shaped like a planet with gold pock marks on the surface and a small hole in the top. We both fell in love with it, named it the Angel Stone and began a game which continues to this day. I was to keep the Angel Stone for some months until something wonderful happened to me, then I was to pass it on to Tony with that energy. He would then keep it and pass it back to me likewise.

I spent a great deal of time meditating on the top floor of my house. Paul Solomon had slept there, and I felt his loving energy with me. I had also held a gathering in the basement to honour an eighty-year-old Japanese Buddhist priestess, Tamosan, and she had chanted magically. The support group I had joined with the Van Cleaves was continuing, and we had developed a 'surround sound' process when one of us was in particular need of tender loving care. We would place that person in the centre of the group, hold them in our arms and sing pure sustained tones. Even with only six of us it was an incredible feeling, like being caressed by the voices of angels. I was beginning to become aware of the power of sound.

At a Soozi Holbeche lecture, I was fascinated to hear her talk about the relation of sound and colour to energy centres. Soozi suggested making a sound mantra from your name, by tuning in to the colour of each letter and giving the colours corresponding sounds. I began to work with my own vowel mantra, chanting it every day, and one morning I took the Angel Stone and placed it on my head, moving it to different parts of my body. Then I sang sound into the hole in the top of it. It felt as though I was coming alive.

So began the process of working with sound on myself. One day I put down the Angel Stone and just emitted pure sounds, focusing the energy on different parts of my body, changing the shape of my mouth to make a 'sound cavern' for the tones to echo around. And then, purely by chance, I made an amazing discovery.

A man I'd been seeing and rather liked had not called me again, and I felt upset. I knew he cared about me, but for some reason was not allowing his emotions to surface. As I did my 'sound meditation' that morning I inadvertently held him and the situation clearly in my mind, and the sound seemed to amplify it. I continued to tone, and my feelings became stronger and stronger. As the sound reached a certain pitch, the word 'alone' jumped into my mind and I felt the tears well inside me. Suddenly, it was as though the intense feelings exploded and I was jettisoned back to my childhood. I saw myself as a small child, standing in front of my father. 'Why do you never show me you care?' I silently asked him. Then a huge release of emotion poured out of me. My heart ached, and I sobbed and sobbed, as I clearly saw a whole chain of men I had drawn to me who could not, or would not, show their feelings. I realized I had chosen those men in the belief I could *make* them love me, but what I was really doing was still trying to heal the situation with my father, trying to make *him* show his love through these men.

It was an amazing revelation, but that was only the beginning. Using a continuing process of sound meditations, I stripped away layer after layer. Not only did I discover I was an emotional onion, but I also realized that problem people and situations in the present were mirroring problems initiated in my childhood, and that if I could release and heal them those situations would no longer affect me in the same way.

I began to perceive the cells of the body as beautiful snowflakes with clear, unbroken patterns. At least, that was how we all started out, but events in our lives distorted and destroyed the delicate patterning, creating debris in the cells. We were carrying emotional trauma in our very cellular structure, and sound could release it!

After working on myself for some time in this way, I shared my ideas with one of our support group, Lizanne Davies, whose flat contained a tiny circular room dedicated to healing. Lizanne suggested we work as a team to experiment with sound, and so the process began. A number of friends came in and out of that room in the guise of guinea pigs, among them my old record producer, John Burgess, now business manager of AIR Recording Studios. John was looking for new premises. As we worked on him that day with sound, I remember gazing out of the window at an old church over the garden wall. Some months later this church was chosen as the new site and, beautifully refurbished, now houses the multi-million pound AIR Studio Complex.

I was intrigued by this healing with sound and the knowledge which seemed to flow through me so naturally. Where did it come from? Had it always been lying dormant within me? Paul Solomon had trained a number of his students in the art of channelling, and Angelica Roquas Hammer offered to do a reading for me. The information she brought through indicated that I had worked with sound before – in Egypt! A priestess in the Temple of Healing, I had orchestrated a choir to use pure tones to heal both individuals and the planet.

I'd always been a practical person and wasn't sure I believed in past lives. Yet at the same time it was good to get confirmation that this healing process with the natural voice was an ancient tradition. I continued to use sound on myself, with good results, although I still had little confidence to try it elsewhere. I was shy, and worried that people would think the sounds I made were odd.

In 1992 I was invited to Dorset with my friend John Christian, to sing at a Paul Solomon gathering. Paul had recently been lecturing in the newly formed Republic of Slovenia, and had returned the hospitality by inviting some Slovenians to England. Over the next few days a great friendship developed between John and me and Darinka Gomišček and Jana Korosec from Nova Gorica. They particularly loved our singing, and asked us to come out to Slovenia later that year.

No one could have been more surprised than I when the invitation materialized into a plane ticket, and I found myself staying with Jana and her husband Stojan close to the Italian border. The invitations continued over the next few years, and I gained a new confidence in my singing and songwriting, performing mainly for patients in hospitals, institutions for mentally and physically disabled people, and schools. I decided to concentrate on writing for theatre and performing my own songs wherever there was an audience to hear me. Everywhere I went in Slovenia, the beautiful heart energy of the people and the countryside seemed to surround and enfold me.

Jana, with her light gold hair, translucent skin and ready smile, had become like another sister to me. She desperately wanted a baby and joyfully became pregnant. But shortly after her son Matej was born in 1994, she died. Our little Slovenian family was devastated. A unique and beautiful spirit, Jana could never be replaced, but a close friend stepped forward to take over organizing concerts and our base moved from Nova Gorica to Ljubljana.

Vesta Vanell was a stunningly pretty woman in her forties who said she had been inspired by the sound of my voice which went through her heart like a laser at the first concert she had attended. She had an immediate and clear vision that my voice had a healing quality which directly opened people's hearts with its high, clear tones. From her tiny kitchen table, which doubled as office desk, filing cabinet and ironing board, Vesta set about planning her 'attack' upon every corner of her homeland, gleefully marking off the towns we 'conquered' with successful concerts, and intently visualizing future sorties for her advancing 'musical army'.

If I had ever had any doubts about my true purpose in being on the planet, this amazing woman quelled them once and for all with her absolute belief in my songs, my voice and my healing abilities. One day she told me that she had had a vivid recollection of living in Egypt and of making me a promise at that time that, when we next met, she would support my work. Past lives again …!

Intrigued to hear about my use of sound on myself, Vesta persuaded me to begin working as a sound therapist on her friends. The interest grew and grew, until one day I found myself standing in front of thirty people with my knees shaking and my throat dry. I was about to teach my first Healing with Sound workshop!

My success in Slovenia as a singer grew side by side with my sound healing, and inspired me to set up some London workshops too. I received so many requests from participants for a book that I realized I would have to write one.

The processes I am about to share with you come from my own intuition and experience. The knowledge was freely given to me and I pass it on to you with love in the hope that it can be used positively to help others. Use it joyfully and with peace in your hearts, and you will discover the amazing secret of sound:

for whatever the sound of your voice, good, bad or indifferent, as you use it to heal others it will purify and energize you in return.

I have presented the techniques very simply (and I hope clearly), with very basic references to musical scales and notation, because healing with sound is something for everyone to use and experience, regardless of whether they have any musical training or expertise. So if you still think you need to be Kiri te Kanawa or Pavarotti to have any effect, take a deep breath. Release it with the sound *ah*. And read on!

Shirlie Roden
London 1998

Chapter 1

WE ARE ALL HEALERS

Have you ever thought how wonderful it would be to have the perfect healing instrument at your disposal, wherever you go, at any time, day or night, to use openly or in secret on yourself, your friends and your family, on children and strangers, the old and the disabled, the sick and the addicted, even animals and the earth? What would you say if I told you you *have* such an instrument and it's yours for life, to use at will? Or have you ever imagined yourself in a stressful situation where you are the one giving positive assistance, calming troubled waters, clearing negative energies and creating harmony? Dream on, you may say! It's all in my imagination. But what if I told you that all of the above is not only possible, but also quite simple to do? Already I can hear your cries of disbelief. 'What, me? A healer? I'm just an ordinary person, nothing special.' I'm going to let you into a secret. We are all ordinary people, and we are all healers. And the most perfect, the most simple and, for me, the most effective healing instrument is something you carry with you for the whole of your life. It is quite simply your own voice.

Why Use the Voice?

But why use the voice, when perhaps you don't feel confident about your sound, or you are a virtuoso on some other instrument or with a different technique? Just think for a moment. There are as many forms of music therapy as there are musical styles. You can take a course on how to listen to and experience classical music in your body. You can bio-dance and release emotions to every rhythm and style and evoke deep feelings with mood music. You can trance-dance and chant with Native Indians and shamans, echo mantras and Mongolian overtones with gurus, drum, chime cymbals, ring bells, gong or be gonged, relax to the flute and the harp, sing with brass sound bowls and clear past lives with crystal bowl vibrations.

But the one thing which is yours alone is your voice. It holds the vibration of your heart energy. It resonates with everything you are in that moment, and it doesn't cost you anything to use it. Your voice is always there at your beck and call, and on the rare occasions when it might disappear, or you don't want to be heard, you can even send its vibrations silently from within you and it will still have a powerful effect.

How Will My Voice Help Myself and Others?

When you think about it, the simplest form of sound healing is probably a mother singing a baby to sleep. Why does it work? Because the mother *cares*. Her heart is open and she is linked in love with her child. That's what you have to do to be a sound healer: let go of your personality and offer your energy in service.

The most instant benefit from sound healing is relaxation. Believe it or not, you can learn to use the pure tones of your voice which, when offered in service, will calm and soothe the recipient, allowing them to let go and drift to magical realms. Basically, all you have to do is put them in a safe, warm environment and use your voice to help relieve pain, stress, trauma and tension. You can focus it on joints, bones, open wounds, skin problems – wherever you feel it's most needed – or you can use it to release painful memories and emotions trapped in the cellular structure of the body and the brain.

CASE STUDY: A Woman With ME/Chronic Fatigue Syndrome

Sandra was a sensitive divorced woman in her fifties, who had been diagnosed with ME seven years previously. When we met, she was experiencing continuous pain throughout her body to the extent that even wearing clothes hurt. She found telephone conversations, prolonged thinking and preparing meals exhausting and was too fatigued to read or write. One day, purely by chance she saw me give a demonstration of sound healing on the television. The sounds I used penetrated her body and travelled up her out-stretched legs 'jangling every nerve'. She said it was like 'wriggling maggots' inside her, and she felt herself literally 'coming alive'. She felt stronger and could breathe and walk better for some time afterwards.

I worked with Sandra over a twelve-month period, using sound to clear her energy centres and counselling to change her thought patterns. Her marriage had gone badly wrong, and she had experienced racial discrimination at work. The ensuing mental and emotional pain had made her want to give up and cut off from life, so she had made a conscious decision to 'close down'. I explained that once she had made the mental decision to do this, it was only a matter of time before the outer physical level followed suit.

My task was two-fold: to release the blocks in her and to rebuild her self-worth. Over the months, I worked with tones to clear programming in various areas. Eyes: her own continuous criticism of herself each time she looked in the mirror Mouth: the unconsciously self-critical words she spoke. Ears: the unsupportive things she had heard people say about her. Throat: the words she'd used to restrict herself through lack of self-worth plus her unexpressed feelings in key situations. Lips: her need to discover her own strength to support herself and speak positively about herself. Her root chakra was completely exhausted, while the second chakra was filled with fear of what might happen in the future. There was a block in her abdomen like a solid stone – all the negative feelings she had experienced within her marriage and withheld, and the solar plexus was full of uncried tears and other people's lies to her.

Sandra responded well from the beginning, saying she felt as though all her bones were clicking back into place as I toned. During sessions, her hands and arms would involuntarily stretch out, sometimes almost moving in harmony with me. After four sessions, the constant pain in her arms and legs had gone. The right side of her body felt perfectly normal, and the left side was improving. Her flat was changing too. Initially, it had felt dark and dead, filled with family photos to give her a sense of belonging, because she never saw her family. I asked her to remove the pictures and begin to love and support herself. We also worked to cut the ties with her family, asking that they begin to honour her and treat her well, and visualized a circle of positive energy around her, to attract positive people.

I worked on her feet, using the laser-like sound to link up energy meridians, intuitively tracing patterns which related directly to the heart and brain. When I knew her body was strong enough, I sent the sound via her feet and central nervous system to the hypothalamus (the HPA Axis) using very high pure notes. Sandra said later it was as though her whole brain and head was filled with sound, which then spread through the entire body.

I knew part of her recovery relied upon her developing a real sense of self-worth, so I lent her Paul Solomon's Self Esteem Survival Kit tapes to listen to. She was becoming aware that she had a choice in the way she thought, and noticed when she went back into old negative patterns. Over a period of five months, as well as the steps forward, Sandra also experienced relapses. Mostly these happened immediately after a sound session and I saw them as a 'healing crisis'. She said the good 'after effects' of the sessions lasted longer and longer, although she was still impatient with her slow recovery and said she was getting fed up with being shut inside.

Eight months after we had begun the sound healing,

Sandra had a big break through and was able to drive her car again and go out socially. Twelve months on from our initial meeting, she now accepts that she has good days when she can move mountains and bad days when she has to allow herself to rest. And whereas every inch of her flesh used to hurt (her words), she now experiences only a slight background ache. She can walk without assistance and has the strength to actively do a string of chores before feeling fatigued. Before, concentration was difficult and she found it hard to understand things and even to speak. Now she feels more like a normal person and is really thrilled with her new mental ability to think differently. She affirms she has improved greatly and is very thankful for the physical healing while also asserting the importance of the support, guidance and counselling she has received.

'Sound healing goes right through the muscle and flesh to the bones,' Sandra told me. 'It's definitely the best way – like ultra-sound only more beautiful.' We continue to work together and as she feels stronger, I always remind Sandra of her part in the process, her courage and commitment to getting better. I hold the image of her shining and radiant in my mind's eye. She is a lovely woman and deserves the health and happiness I believe she will achieve.

Pure voice sound is also an amazing means of communication when a patient cannot speak, or there appears to be no understanding of words. I used it to communicate love to a young man who had just come out of a coma, simply by sitting at his bedside and making the sound *ooh*. His lips could not speak, but his eyes said volumes and finally he managed a smile. Sound is also particularly effective with mentally disabled people. If you just sit with them in the same way and make sound, it seems to get through where logical speech has no meaning. I always feel there's a 'code' in the tones I am making which somehow a part of their brain can understand, because they seem to be fascinated by the sound. There is always immediate eye contact, and it builds a strong link of friendship.

Sound Is the Way Forward

Many people are beginning to say that the foremost method of healing in the new millennium will be sound healing, and science is now proving that the pure sound of the human voice has a healing effect. Dr David Schweitzer's experiments at the Max Planck Institute in Germany tested patients' blood samples before and after singing the sound *ohm* (that is, producing the sound from the belly from a bass note smoothly up three octaves to a high note). After toning, the blood was clearer, brighter and – amazingly – all toxic grey waste matter had been cleared from the blood cells to outside the cells walls. And all this happened after less than a minute of sound, with no pills or potions or surgery or side-effects.

A World of Sound

As I have said, I firmly believe that we all hold healing power within us – we have just forgotten how to use it. So, rather than ask you to learn about sound healing through the pages of this book, I am going to request that, as you read, you merely *remember* what you already know. It is in your genes, and all you have to do is release the knowledge.

When we are born, our intuition and healing abilities function strongly. But as we grow up, we are taught by authority figures to close down what society sees as this rather dangerous and time-wasting area: to stop dreaming, to stop living in the world of our imagination, not to pay attention to that little voice nagging away inside that knows the truth, even when everything else points to the absolute opposite. After all, survival today no longer relies upon our wits, but upon getting the correct qualifications. Sacred sound has very little to do with us.

Or so we think. The truth is that, though we may look solid, we are in fact pure vibrating sound, and the energy of the world we live in today is causing us to vibrate more and more out of tune. Our planet and everything on it vibrates with sound, and many creation myths mention sound as the source of all life. In the Bible, St John's Gospel tells us: 'In the beginning was the

Word, and the Word was with God, and the Word was God.'
The ancient Hindu scriptures, the Vedas, describe creation
beginning with the sacred sound 'ohm', and the sound 'ah'
(which is generally agreed to be the sound of manifestation
from the etheric into the material plane) which is present in
many of the names we use for God across the religious spec-
trum, such as Jehovah, Jahweh, Maria, Buddha, Allah, Ra,
Krishna, Muhammad and Ras Tafari.

Thus in the beginning God sent forth sound, and sound
vibrated against sound at different frequencies, which produced
patterns and structures. As more and more sound poured into
the structures they became denser, eventually creating matter:
sound therefore is the foundation upon which everything is
built, from a human body to a spaceship; and the intricacies of
the interwoven vibrations, if we could but hear them, create a
symphony.

We Have Lost Touch

When we are truly in tune with ourselves and creation, we can
hear this sound. As Native Americans say, the trees and the
ground talk to us. But the speed and materialism of modern life
create dissonance, taking us further and further away from the
natural rhythms of life and from pure unpolluted sound. How
often do we walk barefoot upon the earth, or sit in silence to
listen to the birds singing or the voice of a crystal-clear stream?
We are so bombarded with manufactured sound from cars,
aircraft, machinery, radios, televisions and CD players that most
natural harmonic sound is completely inaudible to us.

And in the Western world we are forgetting how to use our
voices. We used to work together, sowing, reaping, shearing,
spinning, singing work songs to keep time with each other and
the seasons and the natural rhythms of the universe. Mothers
carried their babies on their backs so that the child linked both
to the mother's heartbeat and to the energy of the earth she
worked on.

Yet we still know the power of song. If music is played to cows
being milked, higher yields are produced; plants, too, grow

better under these conditions. Television and CDs may have ousted the old family singalong with Aunty Daisy at the piano, and traditional folk songs and dancing may no longer be taught in many schools, but the popularity of karaoke proves our desire to express ourselves with sound, even if nowadays we need a few drinks before we dare to open our mouths.

A life without balance or rhythm

Over much of our planet modern intensive farming has created an organized landscape in which lone farmers ride tractors over featureless prairies sprayed with pesticides and chemical fertilizers, and where the sound of birdsong, drowned out by both agricultural machinery and road traffic, is diminishing as fast as the birds' food supply of insects. The towns are no better. We complain about the cold and the rain and the heat alike, shutting out nature's cyclic changes instead of living with them, and becoming more and more isolated. In our offices, with the advent of e-mail and computers, it is possible to go through an entire day without speaking to anyone, let alone singing. And our school system, where pupils could benefit so greatly from the emotional release and unifying force of singing, has placed less priority on musical activities compared to other subjects on the curriculum. How can we remain in balance when we are continually programmed to use the logical, left side of the brain at the expense of the right, intuitive side?

Not only is there no time or space for most of us to tune into the natural rhythms of life, but since the discovery of antibiotics at the beginning of the twentieth century we no longer listen to our own bodies. The general belief now is that illness is something that happens to us from outside and can be effortlessly cured with pills. How many people are willing to take responsibility for their thought processes, to believe that there is a direct mind/body link, and that very often we are creating our own illness through the way we think?

The Road to Rediscovery

We need to start all over again, draw a big circle of space and silence around us, and sit inside it for a decade. Then we might actually discover who we really are, what we are here to do and, most importantly, how we are going to do it. But don't worry – I am not going to ask you to lock yourself away in splendid isolation. Five minutes is all we need to begin, and first of all you have to find your voice again.

We're going to start with some very simple practical work which will slowly build with each chapter, so that if you have little or no knowledge of music and singing you will learn as we go, and if you are highly trained you can dip in and out as necessary.

And finally, there is one thing that everyone will experience, whatever your skills: working with sound is fun!

Focus Work

Each day, either when you wake up or before going to bed, spend five minutes in meditation listening to the sound of your body. Go inside the beat of your heart, flow with your blood as it sings through the veins, tune into the pitch of your organs and make sounds with them – any sound that comes to you. Visualize sending sound to different parts of your body, then stop and listen to the silence. Finish by using a sound which is pleasing to you, and visualize light pouring in through your crown, flowing through your entire body, energizing and purifying each cell with the sound.

The Vibration of Your Voice

The sound of the human voice is the most healing instrument of all. The harp can be used for the emotional body, the flute for the mental and the piano to strengthen the will, but the human voice is the most powerful because it carries the heart energy within it. Your voice is literally vibrating with everything you are in this moment and with the pitch and timbre of your speech you are unconsciously sending out signals to everyone you speak to.

Like attracts like, so we draw to us people with similar energy, for the tones of our voice vibrate with both the light and shadow side of us. Life is so perfect that it arranges for our unhealed parts to be mirrored back to us in the people we have attracted, so that we may become aware, heal ourselves and then move on to the next challenge.

But how can I be a sound healer, you may ask, if the negative side of me is vibrating in my voice alongside the positive? Won't it have an adverse effect? The answer is very simple. Learn not to judge yourself. The right and left sides of the brain are constantly chattering to one another, criticizing everything we attempt to do. 'No you can't!' 'Yes I can!' 'You're not good enough.' 'Yes I am.' Someone once described this dialogue to me as Christ (our true potential) being crucified between the two thieves (the two sides of the brain locked in argument). But once we can silence our doubts and centre ourselves, the truth comes shining through and we rise again from the dead.

The amazing thing about sound is that it instantly and perfectly balances the brain and helps create focus. By 'focus' I mean the acceptance of who we are and what we have here and now in this moment.

Stop judging yourself

We are perfect just as we are. Yet we quickly learn to judge ourselves, little realizing that even the sound of the words we use holds an energy which wraps around us. The physical body is a replica of the blueprint in our mind, and we are our own worst critics. If you don't believe me, wait until you start to use sound. You will be amazed at the thoughts which spring into your mind. 'I hope the neighbours can't hear.... I can't possibly help anyone, sounding like this.... His/her voice is much better than mine. I'd better shut up.' These are the kind of statements people make to me in sound workshops, and the same people are amazed when we start working in twos to discover that what they call their 'weedy little voice' is truly appreciated by their partner for its healing qualities! Since the human voice carries the heart energy within it, when you add to that the *intention* to use your voice in service to help, together with loving compassion, the vibration of your voice in that moment will be positive.

How Sound Healing Works

Because sound is the basis of everything, it is the most profound and precise technique for healing and changing the structures and patterns which form our bodies and minds. When I used sound on myself to remove patterns trapped in the cellular structure of my body I perceived that the cells had a memory.

The negative programming of our cells

Most of us are born with good health and beautiful, perfectly shaped clear cells. Then, as we grow, we imitate, and experience, and this is reflected in our bodies. In fact, we begin to experience even *before* birth, taking on thoughts, feelings and patterns from our mothers in the womb. We also carry ancestral and family patterns in our cellular structure.

So what hope do we have of ever being our true selves when we are weighed down by so much programming? The first few years are the most impressionable for a growing child. Everything that happens to him or her emotionally and mentally resonates through the body. Adults imprint a child with experiences of good and bad, right and wrong, love and rejection. In traumatic situations a child invariably believes he or she is to blame, for the authority figure must surely be right. So both this trauma and the associated feelings are sealed inside the child's cells. Rejection, blame, guilt, anger, unlove, worthlessness, abuse – we take it all in, and lock it away.

Throughout life our cells become littered by the debris of pollution, bad diet, stress and lack of exercise, and are distorted with unreleased negative experiences which send out bleeps like microchips in a computer, subconsciously influencing our behaviour. When the cells become completely blocked by this trauma, illness occurs.

'Tuning' the body's cells

So how can sound help us? Think for a moment of the cliché of an operatic soprano and a wine glass. When the singer hits the exact note in pitch and intensity at which the glass is vibrating, the glass smashes. This shows the destrucive element of sound, but also that it can actually change the form of matter.

A Swiss scientist, Hans Jenny, vibrated different sounds on to a metal plate covered with a variety of substances, and beautiful symmetrical patterns emerged. If sound emitted on to sand, water and paste creates universal order, what can it do when used on the human body?

The pure sound of the human voice acts rather like a laser. An intensely focused pinpoint of energy, it penetrates matter and can therefore adjust bone structure (a number of people have reported to me that they heard and felt bones 'click back into place' during sound healing). Pure sound 'tunes' up the cells by vibrating them to a pitch at which negative energy is destroyed or released and replaced by positive vibrations; and where the body is completely out of harmony, it reminds the cells of the sound of perfect health or 'in-tuneness'.

We tend to think of ourselves as having only one body. In fact we have many: physical, mental, emotional, spiritual and etheric. Pure sound is a simple, effective method to clear all of these bodies and has no known adverse side-effects (although very loud high-pitched tones must never be used on chronically ill people, which I will enlarge upon later). Pure sound can also be used to link, clear and energize the nervous system, stimulate the pituitary gland and nourish the adrenals and the immune system.

If this is beginning to sound a little technical, just remember the reality: healing with sound is simplicity itself, and before we go any further we should get back to basics and find out about our own voices.

Focus Work

Sit quietly for a few minutes, close your eyes and tune in to the rhythm of your body organs. Be aware of the breath coming in through your nose, and breathe in through an imaginary channel of air which passes down the back of your throat, goes in between your lungs and ends just below your navel.

Exhale slowly and continue the process for a while, imagining you are breathing in gold light, and breathing out any negative energy. Now, as you exhale, let a humming sound resonate around the back of your nose. Allow the sound to vibrate through your sinuses and cheekbones, down your throat and all the way to your stomach.

Continue with the sound, and when you are ready, on the outbreath, open your mouth and make a vowel sound such as *ah*, *ay*, *or*, *oh*, *ee* or *ooh*. Keep making this sound, raising or lowering the pitch as you wish. Focus your intention very strongly upon the sound and become one with it. Allow every part of your body to melt into the sound until you *are* the sound. Feel it resonate through your whole body, clearing and tuning it, linking it together. Know the power and the purity of the sound that is you. Hold focus and continue to make *your* sound for as long as you like. When you stop, experience the silence again before opening your eyes.

Chapter 2

THE TOOLS OF THE TRADE

The wonderful thing about being a sound healer is that you carry your healing mechanism with you wherever you go, and you can use sound to help immediately in any situation. Even when it is not appropriate to make a noise, you can silently send sound to a person or a group.

The most effective way to work is to be prepared, to take care of your tools. The sound of your voice vibrates with everything you are in a particular moment, mentally, emotionally, spiritually and physically – not only are the cells of your body sending out this vibration, but the electric energy field (or aura) surrounding you is doing so too. A number of things can be done to enable us to work at optimum capacity and enhance the end result.

Your Voice

You do not need a wonderful voice to be a sound healer. Of course, if you can sing in tune and are familiar with the tonic sol-fa system (*doh-re-mi* etc.), it may help, but it is not necessary.

Keep on singing

Whatever your ability as a singer, you need to use your voice in order to strengthen the muscles. This is because using pure sound requires you to repeat tones over and over, and if you are not used to it you may find it tiring at first. So get into the habit of using your voice. Don't strain it or force the sound. Relax your throat muscles, take a deep breath to support your voice, and sing! We don't sing enough. Sing in the garden, in the car, in the house. My mother and I used to sing while doing the mountains of washing up produced by our large family. The perfect place is in the bath, because it creates a natural echo chamber to enhance your voice. Sing to your children, sing at school and at work, sing to old people, sing to your lover, your cat or your dog, the plants, the trees, the mountains, the earth, the stars and the moon. Sing along with CDs and tapes, join a choir, form a folk group, go to church – whatever you like. It's the most wonderful form of emotional release. So get used to using your voice again, to hearing it, experiencing it, knowing it, and appreciating it.

Dietary yeses and no-nos for the voice

Some foods are not helpful if you are serious about being a sound healer. The two main culprits which literally stick in the throat are cheese and chocolate. As a vegetarian I really enjoy cheese, but it is very mucus-forming, so I make a point of not eating it the day before I do a sound healing. (If you want to clear mucus from your throat and nasal passages, eat nothing but brown rice for a week.) In fact, I try to replace all dairy products with a soya equivalent, plus sesame seeds for calcium. After all, cow's milk is a product specifically designed for growing calves. We have to produce a special enzyme, lactase, to digest the sugar in milk and less and less of this is produced as we grow older. If you really love dairy products, goat's and sheep's cheese are easier on the system.

Chocolate is a highly concentrated food, rich in dairy produce, sugar and caffeine, and much as I love the occasional nibble it really does not help the voice. I know people who will eat a bar of chocolate before they go on stage, mistakenly believing the sugar and caffeine will give them a boost. But caffeine causes the body to release adrenalin into the system, producing an unnatural 'high' – a process accelerated by sugar. It takes even more energy for the body to deal with the side-effects of the caffeine and sugar than the chocolate provided in the first place. Result? A net energy loss.

Tea and coffee, containing tannin and caffeine respectively, cause similar problems – again exacerbated if you take sugar with them. If you give them up you may feel sluggish for a few weeks as you experience withdrawal symptoms, but once these are over you will coast along at your own natural energy level.

Whatever the liquid, it does your voice no good if you drink it either ice-cold or boiling hot. And not unexpectedly, excessive alcohol will limit your potential as a healer. Yet many of the soft drinks we consume daily are not really thirst-quenching and are filled with artificial flavourings and chemicals; as a result people can be dehydrated without realizing it.

That's a lot of nos! On the positive side, natural herb teas are great for the voice. And if you want to deal with the dehydration problem and flush your system clean in one fell swoop, just try drinking more water – you may be surprised at how much healthier you feel.

Natural remedies for the throat

Echinacea
You can take this wonderful plant in drops or capsules. It strengthens and boosts the immune system, but loses its powerful effect if taken continuously. I usually take it during the winter, during concert tours, and any time my throat feels sore, so it travels with me at all times.

Grapefruit seed extract
Available as a liquid concentrate, this is a natural antibiotic which I use at the onset of any flu, cold or throat symptoms. It's very bitter, so best mixed with juice, but keep stirring, as the extract is dense and tends to sink to the bottom of the glass.

Ginger tea
This is particularly warming on a cold winter's day and I use it for any throat problems, or while fasting for flu. Grate or chop a

2–3 inch (5–7 cm) piece of fresh ginger root. Slice two lemons and two cloves of garlic. Throw it all in a saucepan, add a pint (560 ml) of water and simmer for twenty minutes. Allow to cool and then add honey to taste. Honey is another natural antiseptic, but its properties are destroyed at high temperatures.

Comfrey tea
Buy a pack of loose leaves from a health food shop and add a few spoonfuls to the ginger tea, or else prepare on its own as a herb tea and sweeten to taste with honey. Comfrey is a renowned healer.

Lemon juice gargle
Only for the brave, but it works! Squeeze a lemon. Taking in a small mouthful at a time, roll the juice to the back of your throat and gargle as long as you can before spitting out. You can also make a saline gargle with salt and water, but be careful not to swallow it.

Garlic
Cooked or raw, it reduces nasal congestion as well as helping to prevent heart disease, some cancers, and cell damage caused by pollutants, radiation and ageing. Since childhood I have had chronic tonsillitis and used to take vast quantities of penicillin. Fifteen years ago I had a very severe attack with a badly ulcerated throat, but this time cured myself by fasting and taking garlic for four days. The cure was magically quick and had none of the side-effects of antibiotics. I haven't had tonsillitis since.

The only drawback with garlic is, of course, the smell. So be careful if you're about to do a sound healing session!

Inhalations
Fill a bowl with boiling water, add a few drops of tea tree oil or olbas oil, place a towel over your head, let the edges cover the bowl, and inhale for as long as you can. The added benefit is that it simultaneously steams clean the pores of your skin. It's great for a chesty cough, too.

Urine therapy

Not for the faint-hearted or squeamish! Drinking your own urine has long been advocated as an energizing homeopathic remedy. I became fascinated one Christmas when I read a magazine article while playing in pantomime, and decided to experiment. For the six months when I drank my own urine (you collect the mid-flow of the first one each morning, but desist if you've drunk alcohol the night before), my breathing and nasal passages were clearer than I've ever known, and my energy level high.

However, be warned: be very careful to whom you divulge your secret. Friends will suddenly bring it up at the dinner table and literally 'take the piss' out of you!

Your tongue

Many people don't know that the tongue is also an organ of elimination for the body, which is why it often becomes 'furred up' and coated during illness. If you fast you will know just how much the tongue can release, because when you abstain from food the body focuses primarily on clearing waste matter and uses old or diseased cells for fuel. You can help this detoxification process by scraping your tongue with a spatula first thing every morning. It also makes your mouth feel delightfully light, clear and healthy and the teeth seem to benefit too. In fact, my dentist continually remarks that I have the cleanest teeth he's ever seen!

The lion posture

This is a yoga posture that sends an extra supply of blood to the throat, also massaging and toning the muscles and ligaments. Sit on your heels (or in a chair) with your hands on your knees, palms face downwards. Take a deep breath, exhale and stick your tongue out as far as possible, simultaneously stiffening your fingers and spreading them far apart. Open your mouth and eyes wide and tense your neck and body, especially the throat. Keep this posture for a few seconds, holding the tension, then relax. Repeat two to three times, or six to ten times in succession several times a day, if your throat is sore.

Reflexology point

There are a number of different schools of reflexology and thus different systems of pressure points. I have been told to use two different reflexology points on the feet for throat and vocal cord problems. The first one is situated in the groove in between the big toe and the first toe. The second is in the groove which separates the underneath of the big toe from the sole of the foot. Apply gentle pressure with your fingers to stimulate these points.

Natural energy enhancers

There are a few perfectly legal substances I can highly recommend to give you energy when you're at a low ebb.

Blue-green algae

Available from any health food shop in powder (mix with juice) or tablet form. A concentrated high-nutrient 'food' guaranteed to give you a boost.

Brewer's yeast

Another booster, available in powder (mix with juice), flakes (add to meals) or tablet form. Contains a high number of B vitamins good for the nervous system and to counteract those destroyed by alcohol. Do not take this if you have candida.

Vitamin C and mineral salts sachets

Available from health food shops in sachet form. Mix with water to make a fizzy energy-booster drink (sweetened with fructose, not sugar). Also good for jet-lag and to recoup mineral losses from excessive sweating.

Essential oil of jasmine

An expensive essential oil, this is my own preference because I actually moisten my fingertips with it and place a little inside my nostrils to inhale! It has a strong, positive, uplifting effect, but before you purchase any I suggest you test yourself to make sure you don't have an allergic reaction. You can of course use any essential oil you like in this way, but in concentrated form these oils are very strong and are not supposed to be applied directly to the skin. Only use a tiny amount and, if your skin reacts adversely, try burning the oil instead. Sometimes when performing I sprinkle the stage area with essential oil, and on occasions I have even cleared and energized the entire auditorium and house seats before the audience has come in.

The Christ quintessence

One of the Master Quintessences available from Aura-Soma (see Useful Addresses), this is a deep red oil with a strong frankincense aroma which is applied to the palms of the hands and inhaled. A highly energizing substance that helps a person to acknowledge his or her life task on earth.

Co-enzyme Q10 or ubiquinone

Taken as a food supplement, this acts as a natural catalyst to help the cells of the body release energy from food. I find it also gives me a great sense of well-being.

Focus Work

You're going to warm up your voice with a few singing scales. The roof of your mouth is divided into two sections. The hard palate at the front acts like a sounding board to vibrate sound-for carrying power and audibility; the soft palate at the back needs to be raised for singing to create a resonant cavity. Do a big yawn and you will feel the soft palate lift. Now sound the consonants 'ng' (as in the word 'lung') a few times and you will feel it moving.

Be aware of your throat, and try to relax it. For a gentle, flowing sound you need to have a passive throat with no tension or strain.

Breathe deeply, down to your stomach, so there is plenty of air to support your voice.

Begin with scales going up from middle C. If you don't have a musical instrument to help your tuning, just start on a note that's comfortable for you, working with tonic sol-fa (singing *doh-re-mi-fa-*

soh-la-ti-doh, up the scale and back down again). Then try the same with *la*, really breathing deeply, working your tongue and opening the mouth wide.

You are going to be using different vowel sounds for healing, so let's start getting used to them now. Sing a scale, experimenting with your lips and stretching them in different shapes, using one at a time the following sounds: *ah, ay, or, oh, ee, ohm*. Try to keep your tongue flat on the floor of your mouth. End with the sound *ooh* and try to create an echo chamber inside your mouth. In the same breath, change from the sound *ooh* to ee and back to *ooh* again. Feel the sound vibrating inside you, and send it up your nose and around your body. You may notice strange-sounding notes creeping in, which are harmonic overtones.

Your Lungs

Every time we take in a fresh breath, we are taking in the opportunity for a new beginning, and when we are using sound to clear and tune ourselves or somebody else, we are literally breathing life and joy into the cellular structure of our bodies. So strong, clear lungs can only be an asset to you. And don't be afraid to use them. You'll be surprised at how much more alive you'll feel with the additional oxygen circulating in you.

Breathing efficiently

With our sedentary lifestyles and polluted air supply, breathing correctly is something we are forgetting how to do. Take in a deep breath right now and see if your shoulders move. They should be relaxed and stationary but many people only breathe from the top half of their chests when they should be inhaling right down to their stomachs.

I find the most efficient way when I am creating pure tones for sound healing is to breathe in through my nose, imagining a channel of air from the back of my nostrils right the way down to my navel, as though I am filling my whole body with air. With most of the exercises in this book, this is what I will ask you to do. However, if you have any sinus problems or find this at all uncomfortable, breathe in through your mouth as this will help to circulate air through all the cavities.

Singing as much as you can, chanting or making any kind of sound will exercise your lungs and increase their efficiency, as will any kind of aerobic activity.

Diaphragm breathing

If you have had singing lessons you will know about diaphragm breathing, a technique used by all trained singers. The diaphragm is a dome-shaped muscle lying across the base of the chest cavity, separating it from the abdomen. As you breathe in, it flattens to enlarge the chest cavity, allowing it to expand and fill with air. As you breathe out, the dome shape reappears to help expel the air. The diaphragm can be trained to expand downwards and outwards to increase the lungs' capacity to draw in and regulate the breath.

Diaphragm breathing is invaluable not only for developing the power of the voice by improving breath control, but also for taking away any strain from the throat. However, it does take some time to master, and although it's a great help for the prolonged toning used in sound healing you can still work perfectly without it.

No smoking, please!

I don't want to point a finger at smokers, because if you do smoke, that's your choice. I was a smoker in my twenties, and became very ill on a Kinks tour in Chicago. It was winter, and walking from an overheated hotel into the bitter air of the Windy City was too much for my chest. I started coughing up foul-smelling tar-coloured mucus so violently that I bruised my ribs. There was a war on: it was either the cigarettes or my lungs.

Happily the lungs won, and I've been without the carbon monoxide, the poisonous tar and the nicotine for over twenty years. What I also discovered when I gave up was how I was using cigarettes to 'suck down' my feelings and suppress my own truth, not to mention drying up my skin and depleting my life force energy. And of course, smoking creates a 'smoke screen' which fills your aura, clings to your clothes and hair, and forms a barrier between you and the subtler healing energies.

Time your meals

One other thing: it's difficult, if not impossible, to sing properly with a full stomach, because you can't breathe deeply. Do try and eat at least three hours before you begin your sound healing session. If it's first thing in the morning and you feel the need for an energy boost, try liquidizing a banana or two with some soya milk and a dash of cinnamon, or mix up a glass of blue-green algae with juice to keep you going.

Focus Work

Stand with your back against the wall to keep your posture upright. Place your hands with palms flat on your ribcage, and bark like a dog. Have fun! You will feel a muscle moving in and out: this is your diaphragm. Now breathe in through the nose right down to your navel as though you were a balloon inflating, and as you do so try to push the diaphragm muscle downwards and out against your hands.

Very slowly, let the air out between your teeth with a ssss sound, attempting to keep the diaphragm muscle pushed outwards. Inhale again through your nose and repeat the process three more times, only repeating the 'dog bark' if you need to relocate your diaphragm.

Now breathe in once more in the same way, allow your throat to relax and slowly release the breath, this time to the sound ah. Try to keep the diaphragm pushed out until all the air is expelled. Repeat the exercise, breathing in to a slow count of four, hold for four, ah for four, until you've done it four times.

Now we're going to sing the alphabet, or as much of it as you can. Breathe in through the nose, exhale singing the letter A. Breathe in again, and this time sing A, B. Then A, B, C, etc. adding a letter with each new breath, until you have sung as far as you can go consecutively with one long breath. With practice, you should eventually be able to sing the entire alphabet in one breath. And don't forget to use your lips like elastic and enunciate clearly!

After these exercises you may feel a little light-headed from the additional oxygen. Sit quietly for a few minutes to allow the energy to circulate through your body and just enjoy the feeling, or drink a glass of water to earth yourself.

Your Body

Recent medical research indicates a direct correlation between the way we think and our state of health, because in an instant our thoughts can produce hundreds of minute chemical changes within the body. In a sense we *are* our thoughts, and, like a self-fulfilling prophecy, we become them, emotionally and physically.

CASE STUDY: Whose Pain Is It Anyway?

Using sound, I took Angela back in time to the point when, as a very small child, she'd intuited her mother's deep fear of a neighbour's ferocious dog, and gone into 'rescue' mode to protect her. From that point on, she unwittingly decided to become responsible for all her mother's anxieties and problems. Little wonder that later in life she went into a counselling profession and almost wiped herself out by focusing so much on other people's problems and pain that she totally ignored her own needs.

Another woman I worked with, Susan, still lived at home with her parents, was chronically fatigued and unable to have a sustained relationship with a man. She had negated her own feelings so much that her heart centre was filled with her mother's emotions and fear of life. Consequently, she was totally unable to express what she herself felt and had been completely taken over by this fear which had affected her immune system, resulting in the fatigue.

The clearer you become from working with sound, the more aware you will be when you unconsciously try to process other people's patterns, emotions and problems. Remember this: we are all responsible only for our own situation and feelings. We are not responsible for what others have created in their lives. Learn the difference between sympathy (subjectively sharing another person's emotion or condition) and compassion (objectively having pity which inclines you to help someone).

Fasting is invaluable

We need to learn to ask our bodies when to eat and what, to go inside the aches and pains and ask them why they're there. Did you ever see a sick animal eating? Animals know instinctively when to fast and allow the body to heal itself, whereas we take a painkiller or antibiotic, block the problem and force ourselves to keep going, which usually only shortens our resistance to further illness.

Fasting is a terrific way to clear your voice, clean yourself out, restore your energy and heal yourself. If I'm ill, I usually fast and take garlic. It's a wonderful antiseptic healer (with the same properties as penicillin, in minute proportions) and has the added bonus of keeping stray vampires at bay!

The give-and-take of healing

Stamina and fitness are important for sound healing, because when you really get into it you may be using your voice for half to three-quarters of an hour, simultaneously stretching your arms in various directions and, depending on how you like to place your patient, kneeling, squatting, crawling or bending for prolonged periods of time. That's the bad news. The good news is that as you use sound to heal others, that sound vibrating through you will also clear, tune and energize you so that you will often finish a session feeling better than when you began.

Eating for general health

We've already talked a little about food and drink. Never forget to bless your food and thank the plants, animals and Earth Mother who provided it for you and helped create the energy for your sound healing. We all now know the basics of a healthy diet: wholegrains and legumes, plenty of fresh vegetables and fruit, limited dairy produce and red meat, even less sugar and processed foods. And organic may cost more, but it's chemical-free and you can really taste the difference.

I've always been wonderful at nurturing others and was surprised to discover, after living on my own for some time, that I was not so good at nurturing myself. Food can be used in so many crazy ways, many of them nothing to do with being hungry. I realized that you cannot honestly and unconditionally give to other people until you have learned to give to yourself, and this reflects right through to the quality of your healing. Now I find equal pleasure in creating those healthy, energizing meals for me alone, or for anyone who's around, and organic wholegrain brown rice is a staple in my diet. It releases energy slowly over a long period of time, so it's great for a late lunch when I've got an evening concert.

Exercise

Some of us are unable to exercise because of the pressures of our daily lives or because of illness or disability, but if you can find a way it can only benefit you. The more oxygen you take in to clear out the old air, the better you will feel and the greater will be the capacity of your lungs. Whether it's swimming, running, the gym, aerobics or yoga, find out what works for you. I do a mixture of everything, but my bible is a little book called *Tibetan Secrets of Youth and Vitality* from which I learned five simple ancient Tibetan exercises to perform daily. It takes very little time and really seems to awaken and strengthen me.

Focus Work

Make a list of everything you eat and drink during one day. Note when and where you eat it, and the surrounding physical and emotional circumstances. Study the list and discover how you can nurture yourself better not only with the foods you consume but also through the atmosphere you choose to eat in. What foods make you feel really good, and what are the 'trigger' foods you turn to under stress? How can you create a more peaceful and harmonious environment in which to nourish yourself on all levels?

Write down two or three intentions for yourself, such as 'I intend to truly love, honour, nurture and support myself on all levels'. For the next few weeks try to focus on them before going to sleep and when awaking.

When you've written down your intentions, sit quietly in a meditative posture and focus on your breathing. Keeping your eyes closed, visualize with your mind's eye that you are surrounded by gold light. Now imagine you are breathing it in, and see it flowing like gold blood through your veins, energizing and healing every part of your body. Now begin to make a sound, intuitively choosing the pitch and vowel, and visualize that sound flowing round your body with the gold light. See the sound penetrating the cells of your body until even the nuclei are pulsing with it and the cells are tuned to perfection, emitting pure gold health and energy. Now alter the pitch of the sound until you are singing the lowest note you can, linking it to the base of your spine. Hold the thought in your mind, 'Every cell in my body is now vibrating with perfect health.'

Imagine the vertebrae of your backbone are like the ivory keys of a piano. Breathe in deeply and slowly begin to move your low tone up the octaves in pitch to the highest note you can sing, visualizing the sound moving up your backbone to the crown. Do this as smoothly as you can, and repeat three or four times. When you stop, sit for a moment in silence, and experience the energy flow in your body, before you open your eyes.

Your Spirit

The more you can free yourself from your patterns, let go of your ego and open yourself up spiritually to your higher self, the more you will be able to act as a pure vessel for healing energy to flow through. The simplest and quickest ways of opening are through meditation and prayer. There are as many forms of meditation and as many different prayers as there are religions, and it is up to you to discover what works for you in the context of healing.

Meditation

We live in a world of so many stresses and pressures, both emotional and physical, that we owe ourselves a quiet half-hour at least once a day. If you can't find a local meditation group there are many cassettes on the market to guide you. Or you can try a simple technique such as focusing on the flame of a lighted candle, allowing your thoughts to surface, letting them float away and focusing on the candle again.

Another way is to use an intricately patterned mandala to focus on, or a flower or tree or mountain. Alternatively you can try closing your eyes and going inside yourself, as we have already done in some of the earlier focus work. Create your own mantra with a word like 'peace', or a sound you like. Repeat it silently over and over in your head, allowing your brain to centre on the sound. If you have thoughts, follow them through, let them go and return to the sound or word.

Anything you can do to release tension and relax yourself, to place you back in the flow of the cosmos, can only benefit all areas of your life. Many people think they haven't got time to meditate, but I find it centres me so much that afterwards I do everything with twice the speed, efficiency and clarity.

Prayer

I have included prayer in this section not for religious reasons but because it forms part of the ritual of my sound sessions and my daily life. It is a wonderful way of giving thanks and sending out blessings, because simple honest prayer really opens and touches the heart. And it works. One inspiring way of praying and meditating simultaneously is chanting, which is also great for clearing old energies, revitalizing space and filling your energy field or aura with positive vibrations.

Focus Work

Have a clock in your sight to time this following exercise. Sit in a comfortable position, close your eyes and focus as usual upon your breathing. Bring into your mind all the positive aspects of yourself: your abilities, gifts and talents, the essence of what makes you such a special individual. As you breathe, really experience in your body the vital energy of these positive qualities.

Now you are going to try to chant for at least ten minutes, using the words *I am*, and if at any time you want to add another word to the chant (such as *I am love*, or *I am peace* or *I am joy*), please do. Breathe in through the nose to your stomach and exhale a few times, then begin to chant, making the syllables *I am* as long or as short as you wish.

Continue for ten minutes if possible, allowing the sound to resomate through your body and empower you. When you have finished, sit in silence for a few minutes more and feel the energy in your body before you open your eyes.

Chapter 3

SACRED SPACE

You've started the practical work on yourself, and should by now be accustomed to your own sound and its effect on your body and emotions. According to the Vedas, the vibration of sound travels the universe seven times and then settles within it, so when we utter sacred sound we are actually adding to the banks of positive energy and helping to combat the negative sounds emanating from the more materialistic side of human nature. But before your sound reaches out into the universe it will affect your immediate environment, 'soaking' into the woodwork and bricks. So if you can create a 'sacred space' dedicated to your sound healing, so much the better: the positive vibrations will accumulate.

Setting Up a Room for Healing Space

If you don't have a spare room, designate an area of your living space. A wooden floor is useful, because it can act as a 'sound board' and intensify the experience; but again it isn't essential. Try to keep the area as free of clutter as possible. Remember, even objects emit sound vibrations, and while working with sound, *you* are the sacred object. Do you really need that pebble from Glastonbury and the replica of the Egyptian Sun God before you can channel the light? Don't give your power away before you've even experienced it!

Be aware also of noise. Do the windows overlook the street

and reflect the sound of traffic? Do people constantly walk past the door, chattering? Where is the telephone? All these things can conflict with the pure sound you are making and interrupt the healing process.

It is also up to you to decide how you want to orchestrate your sound sessions. I like to have a mattress at floor level for patients, but you may prefer something at table height. But bear in mind that it's useful to be able to move freely around your patient from all angles.

You can 'clear' your space or room in a number of different ways. I like to use sage sticks (dried bundles of herbs used by Native Americans to 'smudge' or cleanse), and make prayers and affirmations as I waft smoke into every corner. You can also use a clear brass bell, a drum or a rattle to move energy; or simply clap your hands loudly and chant; or you might like just to sit in the centre and use your own voice to send pure sound around the room; or you can bless some water and sprinkle it around with your hands or a feather.

Once this process is completed I like to add some fresh flowers, because they have such a bright, joyful vibration of their own. You will need a candle for lighting, and it's also a good idea to have a glass of water handy in case you get a tickle in your throat while toning. My constant companions when making sound are paper and pen, because sound opens my intuition so much that the ideas pour through me, in the form of either creative inspiration when working on myself, or perceptions and messages when working on others. Always have tissues handy – sound really does release the emotions! – and a blanket. Even in a centrally heated room, patients may feel cold as energy begins to move.

Feng Shui

You can also fine-tune your healing space by applying some basic principles of Feng Shui. Based on the ancient Chinese *I Ching* oracle, this popular art claims that the layout of your living area can affect your relationships, your finances and your health. A Ba Gua or grid, which is divided into different areas reflecting various aspects of your life, is placed over the floor

Feng shui Ba Gua

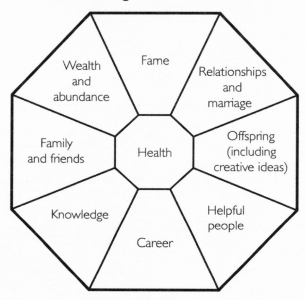

plan of whatever you wish to feng shui – your home, your office, a plot of land, a patio or even a table – and the contents and layout of each area are adjusted accordingly to release blockages and enable energy to flow freely.

By placing the Ba Gua so that the Career area is directly in line with your front door or entrance hall, you can see which areas of your living space correspond to which aspects of the grid. Thus the area as you directly enter represents Career. To your left is Knowledge, to your right Helpful People and so on. Most of us don't live in perfectly rectangular spaces, so when areas are missing framed mirrors can be placed on the relevant walls to reflect the energy back in symbolically.

Things to be aware of range from toilets in any area (flushing away that quality, so keep the lid and door closed), to waste-paper baskets (throwing away that quality) and piles of papers, junk or rubbish in cupboards, which block the energy flow. Positive assets are flowing water such as ornamental waterfalls and fish in tanks (particularly good in the Wealth area), wind chimes to slow energy along long corridors, healthy vibrant plants (with round rather than spiky leaves, because they give off a welcoming energy) and multi-faceted crystals, which are wonderful hung in windows to reflect sunlight and create rainbows. Check what symbolic ornaments and pictures you put where – for instance, if you are looking for a new relationship, don't have single objects in that area. Try something in pairs, or a beautifully radiant painting which inspires you. Colour can also be used to raise the vibration or calm it down accordingly.

Study the Ba Gua in relation to your whole house, flat or living area, and use it to help you decide exactly where to create your healing space. Then stand in the entrance to your healing space, holding the grid so that the Career area is in line with the door to this room and Helpful People again to your right with Knowledge to your left. Now you can see what to place in which area of your healing space. For instance, if you want to be famous as a healer, put a chart or poster to do with healing in the Fame area on the wall directly opposite you. If you have a guru or spirit guide, they can go in the Helpful People area. Your patients can lie in the Health area, and so on. Be creative, and remember what I have already said about clearing the clutter and allowing free flow of energy.

Crystals

These can be an asset with sound, because they can be programmed, but do remember whenever you acquire a new one to cleanse it before using it. Clear quartz is the easiest to programme, and the simplest way is to soak the crystal for twenty-four hours in still spring water laced with a good tablespoonful of natural sea salt. I have a large solid block of clear quartz that has travelled the world with me for many years and likes to sit beside me while I emit sound, but I rarely use crystals during my healing sessions.

Here are a few ideas to experiment with. Before you begin, always remember to purify yourself with a prayer and ask the Angels of Sound to sing with you. More on that below.

Crystal octave

Take eight crystals, cleanse them, and tune each into a note in the musical scale until you have completed a full octave. That is, using a tuning fork or a tuned musical instrument to find the right pitch, start at middle C (*doh*) with the first crystal, singing the note over and over as a pure sound mantra, transmitting the vibration of that sound from your voice into the crystal. When you intuitively feel this is completed, start on the next crystal with the musical note D (*re*), and continue up the tones (E, F, G, A, B: *mi*, *fa*, *soh*, *la*, *ti*), finishing with the C (*doh*) an octave above middle C.

When each crystal has been programmed with a musical tone, place them in a large circle on the floor, beginning with middle C and keeping the order of the tones. You can then sit inside the crystal circle for your sound meditation, and it will anchor the Angels of Sound to guide you in your work. You can also place your patient inside the circle for the healing session, and even rotate them if you wish, because the crystals will simultaneously transmit the tones and enhance the auric field of that person.

Crystal mantra

While working on a patient, you may have discovered that a particular sound seems to affect them beneficially. Using the technique above of singing over and over into a previously cleansed crystal, you can charge it with the healing sound they need, and give it to them to carry about. The crystal will keep transmitting this specific sound vibration and continue the healing process you initiated at the session. You can also charge a crystal with sound for yourself, or as a special gift for a friend.

If the person is not present, ask to be 'given' the right note to use, and sing it repeatedly into the crystal. You are not limited to using one sound: others can be added on top, but if you're going to do this please ensure the additional notes are perfectly in tune with the first one or you will create dissonance rather than harmony, which will then be amplified by the crystal. Never add extra tones at a later date (unless you have perfect pitch), as you cannot be sure they will be in tune with the original note.

Angels of Sound

Yes, there are Angels of Sound, and yes, we are going to be working with them. Or maybe it would be truer to say *they* are going to be working with *us*, because the final choice is theirs. Everybody has their own healing angel who is with them at their birth and guides them throughout their lives, but generally we don't allow ourselves the time or space to experience this beautiful and immensely loving energy.

When I say we'll be working with angels, I don't mean you'll actually see them standing in the room (unless you're particularly clairvoyant), although you very possibly will see them in your mind's eye. With practice, you will learn to tune into them intuitively and feel their gentle guidance giving you the correct tones, telling you when to move where, and leading your hands from one part of the body to the next. And if you really dedicate yourself to sound healing, you'll hear their voices on occasions joining in with yours. Sometimes, when you open your mouth to sing, it will feel as though your voice has disappeared and pure sound is pouring forth instead, like a swirling coloured stream of energy. That's when you know the angels are singing through you.

You can also learn to work with the angels as though they were assistants in a surgical operation, handing them energy forms you have removed with sound, and receiving from them gifts such as 'seeds of love' to plant in various chakras as blessings, ready to grow into full-bloomed flowers. I will expand on this later.

CASE STUDY: A Gift from the Other Side

Diane was a high-powered businesswoman in her forties who worked in a competitive man's world, and the first thing I felt when I used sound on her was that she had put all her energy into her breasts for safe keeping! I tried to rebalance the energy, drawing it down to her ovaries, and was not surprised to learn later that she had been diagnosed with growths in her abdomen. I was aware of an unhealed situation with her father which had affected her relationships with men, and towards the end of the session I 'saw' an old woman standing at Diane's feet. She was holding a fluffy white toy dog which she was offering to Diane as a token of love.

I am used to all kinds of 'visitors' when working with the Angels of Sound, but even so my logical mind said this was taking things a little too far. However, the old woman persisted, so eventually I reached out into empty space, 'took' the imaginary dog and placed it on Diane's heart centre.

As we talked after the session, I tentatively asked Diane if she had ever had such a toy as a child, because an old woman had now sent her one as a gift. Diane's eyes filled with tears. Her parents had split up when she was small and her father had given her ... a small fluffy white toy dog! This had become a symbol of his love and had gone everywhere with her. However, as it got tattier and tattier a sharp piece of metal began to protrude from it, and her grandmother had taken it from her and destroyed it. Diane had felt devastated, as though she had lost her father's love.

When I told her that her grandmother had given her back the toy dog, the 'inner child' in Diane which still felt sadness from the loss of her father was greatly healed. Her devastation was replaced by a deep sense of feeling loved through the grandmother's gift, which simultaneously asked forgiveness of Diane and showed her she was still loved and supported by those now in spirit.

Invocations and prayers

Before I begin my sound sessions, I always light a candle and make a prayer of attunement and invocation to the angels. Again, it's up to you to be creative, so your prayer can be anything you like. But make it powerful; as there are Angels of Sound, so there are also Angels of Dissonance. At the time of creation these mischievous angels distorted some of the pure sound into discord, and while the Angels of Sound now work to create harmony on all levels, the Angels of Dissonance have great fun bending out of key any pure sounds which are not strong. So understand what you are working with, because wherever you create a bright light, darkness is attracted to put it out. But if you allow yourself the vision, trust and strength to create a shield of protection with your prayers, there is nothing to be afraid of. Command the Angels of Dissonance to leave and sound a pure sound, and they will stay away anyway – the one thing they can't stand is pure, tuneful sound!

As I light my candle I make a simple dedication to call in the light, and ask anything that is not in the light to be removed from the room. I then offer mysef as an open channel of service and ask the Angels of Sound to work through me, waiting until I feel the connection, and then personalizing it by requesting the specific angel of the person I am healing to sing through me. My final invocation is to call upon the energy of Christ the Healer and Mary the Compassionate Mother, to balance the masculine and feminine within me as I work.

At the end of your sessions, don't forget to blow out the candle and thank the Angels of Sound for working with you. They will be happy to return to a place where they can be of help, and are honoured and appreciated, and the more you call them to you, the more their energy will vibrate through your sacred space.

Focus Work

Locate a room or place in your home which feels right to use as your sound healing space. Using any of the methods above, cleanse and clear the energies in this space and decide how you are going to use it (mattress, cushions, massage tables etc.) and what sacred objects you will allow into it. Devise and write out your own prayer of protection and invocation of whatever positive energies you wish to call in, ending with the Angels of Sound. Sit in your space, call your own Angel of Sound to you, intuitively choose a note and vowel sound, and gently emit the tone as purely as you can, trying to create what you imagine is the purity of the original sound of creation. Don't judge yourself, and don't worry if the sound isn't perfect. Use your lips and the shape of your mouth to alter the sound until it feels as though it is streaming from your mouth like a pure river. Feel the closeness of your angel making the sound with you. Continue as long as you like, and when you have finished thank your own angel and the Angels of Sound.

The Sacred Space Within

How many times have you heard the saying 'Your body is a temple'? When you begin to work with sound, you also begin truly to understand what this means. The Swiss scientist Hans Jenny, I mentioned earlier, discovered that when the sound *aum* or *ohm* was sung into an electronic transmitter the sound-waves created an intricate star-like pattern, virtually identical to a yantra used for centuries in the East to represent the *aum*. A yantra is a complex concentrated visual linear image used for meditation.

If we break down the sounds of *aum*, we have *ah* for the grounding, earthing, anchoring of creation, *u* or *o* (because *u* turns into *o* as it leads into the *m*) for the vibration of eternity, and *mmmm* for the movement of sound. This is why *aum* is called the mantra of mantras, the sound of the beating of God's heart, in perfect equilibrium: because it contains everything there is.

Bearing in mind the perfect pattern the sound *aum* can create, you might like to consider the origin of the beautiful designs in plaster, mosaic and coloured glass in the ceilings, floors and windows of old churches, temples and sacred places as a kind of out-picturing of the sacred and harmonious sounds which have been sung and chanted over the centuries.

So when we begin to use sound on ourselves, we are creating these perfect patterns within us. When I first experimented on myself I had a vision of the cells of the body as perfect snowflakes whose intricate structure had been destroyed and damaged by our own disharmonious behaviour and lifestyle. I saw that by using sound the 'snowflakes' could be rebuilt, because we cannot make sacred sound ourselves without a corresponding manifestation in every atom of our being. The vibrations of the sounds we use (as with the *aum* creating electronic sound-wave patterns) will out-picture inside us.

Thus, using sound, we are capable of creating the temple within, and retuning every cell to the sound of perfect love. This is the temple to which you can call the Angels of Sound – the temple of your inner wisdom where you can rest in peace and listen to your higher self.

Focus Work

Light a candle, make your prayers and invocations, and sit quietly in your sacred space. By now, you should be aware of the special energy of this space from the sound you have been using in it. Following your breathing, envisage that sacred space opening inside you. Intuitively choose a pitch and vowel sound and begin to sound a tone, imagining as you do the space inside you becoming clear, perfect and harmonious.

As you continue to tone, allow that space inside you to grow until it fills your body and spreads out into your aura. See yourself as a beautiful empty temple. Create beautiful gold bells hanging above your head, and when you feel ready, sound a bell to call the Angels of Sound to you. Ask the angels to sing with you, through you and around you, and continue your sound as long as you like, allowing it to fill and vibrate every area of the temple you have created.

When you have sung enough, thank the Angels of Sound and slowly shrink the temple, drawing in your energy until the temple is small enough to sit safely inside your heart. Come out of the temple, close the door with a blessing and walk away, gradually allowing yourself to return to the space behind your eyes before opening them.

You can return to the temple at any time, and once you become accustomed to visiting it you can call it into your consciousness at any moment as a safe place for the Angels of Sound to work with you.

Warming Up the Temple of Sound

We've been up on the spiritual planes for quite a while, so now we're going to come solidly back down to earth and address the physical aspect of the temple: your working body. As all singers and actors know, for a good performance you must warm up properly first. Everything we've done so far has been a rehearsal for our 'opening night', so before we actually walk out on to the healing stage and face the crowds and the critics here are a few exercises to get the energy flowing and help your voice.

Top-to-toe-let-go

Stand with your feet shoulder-width apart, knees slightly bent, and slowly allow your torso to bend over as far as it will comfortably go, arms hanging loosely, until almost touching your toes. Now make a low-pitched continuous sound, letting the pitch go higher and higher like a factory hooter going off, as you simultaneously move your torso and arms to an upright position until the arms are stretched right above your head. Hold the position, take in a deep breath and exhale with any sound you like. Take another deep breath, make a high-pitched continuous sound and slowly begin to collapse your body to the touch-toes position again, this time taking the pitch in a down-ward curve. As you reach the touch-toes position, allow everything you want to let go of emotionally and physically to come out in the sound. Repeat three times.

Energize and cleanse

Hold your arms outstretched, fists clenched. You are going to pull your fists towards your chest, as though pulling in energy with four sharp pulls, and simultaneously breathe in through your nose with four sharp intakes of breath. On the fourth breath, when your fists reach your chest, hold. Then expel the air through your mouth with four sharp breaths like a steam engine, and four sharp fist pushes outwards until your arms are extended. Repeat three times. Imagine you are pulling in energy with the inbreaths and expelling toxins with the outbreaths.

Tongue twisters

These are great for warming up your lips and your sense of humour. Really try to stretch your lips and enunciate clearly when doing them. My favourites are 'Red lorry, yellow lorry' and 'I am the very model of a modern major general, I've information vegetable animal and mineral', as fast as I can. Sing your chosen phrase on one note and then repeat, moving up a tone to the next note, until you have gone up and down an octave. Don't forget to breathe! You can also make up your own exercises incorporating all the vowel sounds, such as 'Easy rider rode the ranges on his useful pony' or 'Eagle soaring high in the sky, are you going my way?'

Musical scales

If you haven't got the time or inclination for any of the above, try to sing a few musical scales (*doh-re-mi*) to warm up your voice before you begin your sound session. Any of the exercises in the Focus Work are fine, or you can create your own. Counting from one to ten to extend breathing is also good (same process as with the alphabet: one, then one two, then one two three etc.) and you can also try laughing like a lunatic (a great energizer!), letting the laughs go up and down the scale. Just find something that you enjoy doing.

Hand massage

You're going to be using your hands a great deal for directing 'laser beams' of sound and colour. Although the sound issues from your mouth, you will soon begin to experience it as an energy flowing from your fingertips and palms as well. Think of your nervous system like a map inside you, with energy pathways or meridians linking different parts of your body. If you bear in mind that the heart is linked to your arms and hands, you can envisage your hands as an extension of that heart energy. A short massage can help to release any blockages in these areas.

Using the thumb and first finger of the hand you're not working on, gently pull your other thumb (the life-force energy) from base to tip as though you were pulling your life-force energy up. Then squeeze hard on the tip of the thumb and nail. Massage down the thumb, working the joints well, then squeeze the flesh between thumb and first finger (what would be the webbing in a frog), massaging well.

The fingers reflect mental and emotional states. One by one pull them upwards, squeezing the tip of each finger and nail, and massaging the joints in the same way, not forgetting the skin in between each finger, until you have done each hand. Bend your fingers gently back as far as you can, pull again, and see if you can crack any of the joints.

Finish by rubbing both palms hard together. Place your cupped palms over your eyes (always good if they're feeling tired). You'll be surprised how much energy you can feel. Breathe it in and repeat this 'palming' process as many times as you like.

We've covered a lot of ground together, but now you're ready to begin. You've learned that a light, pure diet, together with meditation and exercise, will help you create a refined, attuned, balanced physical instrument; you've realized that if, like a Stradivarius violin, you are made with loving care from natural materials, you will resonate with a beautiful tone and a special quality of heart. So now you really can start to see yourself as an acutely sensitive musical instrument, ready to play the music of God.

Because, you see, it will be your intention as a sound healer to create, maintain and strengthen the pure sounds of mankind, and to harmonize every aspect of each physical body you work on. Are you really ready? Of course you are. By sounding pure sound, we are going to call into being our Light Bodies. It's as simple and as amazing as that.

Chapter 4

SOUND, COLOUR AND MOVEMENT

If you have the *Sound Healing* cassette tape or CD (see p. 177), this is where you will begin to use it.

There are as many different systems of sounds for healing as there are teachers, and the following system is one I have intuitively developed over several years. Knowledge is universal, and I only refer to this system as 'mine' in the sense that it works for me and achieves the desired results. If you want to use a different system, please do, and if you want to align different sounds and colours to different energy centres, feel free. Use your intuition: I am only giving guidelines, and what feels good to me may not necessarily suit you.

The Chakras

Most disciplines agree that the body has seven main energy centres called 'chakras', from the Sanskrit word meaning 'wheel'. Working up the spine, they are root (base of the spine), sacral (just below the navel), solar plexus (upper abdomen below rib cage), heart, throat, third eye (centre of forehead between eyebrows) and crown (pate of the head). Because these energy vortices rotate at different speeds, each vibrates with a different colour and emits a different sound. In fact, most of the organs of the body have their own sounds and some teachers have allocated a precise musical note in pitch to each organ. I prefer to believe that different people at different stages of development and health are vibrating at their own individual frequencies, and so I always advocate using your intuition to find the right note.

These energy centres or chakras open at various stages in our lives, and by the time we are twenty-two should all be functioning at optimum level. However, due to our modern lifestyles, it is rare for all the chakras to be simultaneously clear and open. Painful situations and stress cause us to close down. Many people feel they can only deal with their problems by shutting them out or holding them tightly inside. But this has the opposite effect, blocking the chakras so the life-force energy cannot circulate freely through our bodies: and blocked energy results in aches, pains and ultimately illness. Pure sound directed at the chakras acts immediately to stimulate, harmonize and clear the energy.

You are now going to begin to use sound on yourself in a very simple way, moving up the energy centres of the body from the root chakra to the crown in three stages: firstly with sound, secondly with sound and colour, and thirdly with sound, colour and movement. This is so you can gradually become aware of what each centre feels like, where it is placed in the body, and how you can change the energy with sound.

Energizing Sounds: Chakra Chart

Sound	Chakra	Note	Sol–fa
I am	whole body	C	*doh*
ooh	crown	B	*ti*
ohm	third eye	A	*la*
ee	throat	G	*soh*
oh	heart	F	*fa*
or	solar plexus	E	*mi*
ay	sacral	D	*re*
ah	root	middle C	*doh*

Before we begin, look at the chakra chart to familiarize yourself with these centres and their corresponding sounds. I have included the notes of the musical scale and tonic sol-fa next to each sound because it is good to start each sound session with an octave of notes – moving from a low note at the root of the scale to a high one at the top. Sounding an octave helps to lift the energy in the body. If you are not working with my sound tape or a musical instrument, it is not essential to pitch perfectly. But to experience the sense of 'pulling the energy up through you' with sound, you need to start with a low note that feels good to you and move up the musical scale tone by tone with each chakra.

For the best results stand up, but if you're unable to do this you can still experience the sounds by closing your eyes, relaxing with your breath and sitting comfortably. If you have any problems inhaling through your nose, breathe through your open mouth.

Using Sound on Yourself

With these systems we shall be moving energy from the base of the spine to the crown of the head, clearing blocks and invigorating ourselves as we go. You can use any or all of the systems as a release, a warm-up, an energy tune-up or a sound meditation (sit comfortably for this), and in Chapter 7 I will explain how to use it for creative writing.

The individual sounds can be used by themselves for healing, on either the relevant chakras or whatever part of the body you are drawn to. Follow your instinct – does a high sound feel good, or a low one, and what vowel? Learn to work with colour as well: if, in your mind's eye, a chakra is emitting too much of one particular colour, you can draw it out using a sound; and if you intuit that another chakra is lacking in colour, you can send this colour in with the sound.

You will also discover favourite sounds to which your body responds. One woman came in on the second day of a workshop, completely transformed by using the sound *I am* that morning. Chanting it for twenty minutes had magically cleared all her negative feelings and she was full of new energy. What works for someone else may not necessarily work for you: but rest assured, *something* will work for you. It's up to you to discover what the sound is.

Energizing sounds

Stand straight, with your feet shoulder-width apart, arms hanging loosely by your sides, knees slightly bent. If you're sitting down, uncross your legs and place your hands palms downwards on your thighs. Relax and breathe in. Focus on the root chakra at the base of the spine. When you sing, open your mouth wide, relax your throat, uncurl your tongue and allow it to rest on the floor of the mouth.

Ah: We're going to start with the energizing sound *ah*, breathing the energy in through the nose, pulling it up through the base chakra and singing on the outbreath. Breathe in and exhale with the sound *ah* for a slow eight counts. Repeat three times.

Ay: Now breathe the energy up through the nose from the root chakra to just below the navel. Moving up the musical scale to the next note, we're going to use the breath to clear the blocks in the digestive system. Widen your mouth, breathe in and exhale with the sound *ay* for a slow eight counts. Repeat three times.

Or: This time as we breathe in, we're going to pull the energy up from the navel to the solar plexus, clearing problems and allowing us to let go of fear. Form your lips into a small circle, breathe in and exhale with the sound *or* for a slow eight counts. Repeat three times.

Oh: Use your breath now to move the energy up from the solar plexus right into the heart centre, opening the heart and letting in love. Still keeping your lips in a small circle, open your mouth a little wider. Breathe in and exhale with the sound *oh* for a slow eight counts. Repeat three times.

Ee: Breathe the energy up from the heart into the throat centre – the centre of your willpower, where you speak your truth. Stretch your lips wide, breathe in and exhale with the sound *ee* for a slow eight counts. Repeat three times.

Ohm: Now we're going to breathe the energy up from the throat into the third eye centre on the forehead between the eyebrows – the centre of your intuition. Open to your intuition with the sound *ohm*, beginning with *oh* ending with *m*. Let the *m* resonate on your lips. Breathe in and exhale with the sound *ohm* for a slow eight counts. Repeat three times.

Ooh: Now breathe the energy up once more from the third eye to the crown, opening to universal knowledge. We're going to use a pure clear sound to create clarity and purpose. Breathe in and exhale with the sound *ooh* for a slow eight counts. Repeat three times.

I am: Breathe the energy in now through your whole body – through every nerve, muscle, tissue and pore. Feel the breath of life flowing through every cell, energizing and relaxing you. Breathe in and exhale with the sound *I am* for a slow eight counts. Repeat three times. Allow the energy to circulate so that even the nuclei of your cells are tingling. Feel the vibrancy. Sound yourself alive!

Colourful sounds

Now we're going to repeat the process, this time adding the energy of colour. Before we begin, study the Colourful Sounds chart. We are simply moving through the colours of the rainbow, with the addition of pure white for focusing on the whole body.

Stand straight, with your feet shoulder-width apart, arms hanging loosely by your sides, knees slightly bent. If you're sitting down, uncross your legs and place your hands palms downwards on your thighs. Relax your body and throat and breathe in. Focus on the root chakra at the base of the spine and imagine a vibrant red colour, like a beautiful poppy, filling this chakra with life and vitality.

Ah: You're going to breathe in the colour red until the whole of your base chakra is awake and alive, and on the outbreath energize your fire. Breathe in the colour red to the root, and exhale with the sound *ah* for a slow eight counts. Repeat three times.

Colourful Sounds: Chakra Chart

Sound	Chakra	Colour
I am	whole body	white
ooh	crown	purple
ohm	third eye	indigo
ee	throat	blue
oh	heart	green
or	solar plexus	yellow
ay	sacral	orange
ah	root	red

Ay: Now breathe in again through the nose. As you pull the energy up from the root to the sacral chakra, just below the navel, see the red change to a strong orange, like a glowing marigold, the colour of joyful new beginnings. Breathe in orange to the sacral chakra, and exhale with the sound *ay* for a slow eight counts. Repeat three times.

Or: Now breathe the energy up from the navel to the solar plexus, the centre of the sun, as the orange changes to golden yellow like a sunflower, giving us the confidence of unlimited possibilities. Breathe in yellow to the solar plexus and exhale with the sound *or* for a slow eight counts. Repeat three times.

Oh: Breathe in once more, this time drawing the energy up from the solar plexus right into the heart centre, as yellow turns to a healing, harmonious green, like soft green foliage. Breathe in green to the heart and exhale with the sound *oh* for a slow eight counts. Repeat three times.

Ee: Now breathe the energy up from the heart, this time into the throat centre with the colour blue, like crystal bluebells, for truth and clear communication. Breathe in blue to the throat, and exhale with the sound *ee* for a slow eight counts. Repeat three times.

Ohm: Now we're going to breathe the energy up from the throat into the third eye centre on the forehead, as blue changes to indigo, like deep blue violets, and we open to our inner seeing and wisdom. Breathe in indigo to the third eye, and exhale with the sound *ohm* for a slow eight counts. Repeat three times.

Ooh: Now breathe the energy up from the third eye to the crown. The indigo changes to soft violet, like a gentle purple iris, the colour of universal love, as we walk the path of transformation. Breathe in purple to the crown, and exhale with the sound *ooh* for a slow eight counts. Repeat three times.

I am: Finally, breathe the energy in through your whole body: through every nerve, muscle, tissue and pore. See the purple change to pure white light, cleansing you, clearing you and revitalizing you to be your true self, like a beautiful pure white lily. Breathe in white through the whole body, and exhale with the sound *I am* for a slow eight counts. Repeat three times.

Moving sounds

By now you should be getting used to the sound which corresponds to each body centre. This time we're going to add arm movements, which will open up the body and allow the energy to flow even more. Study the Moving Sounds chart before you begin, to familiarize yourself with the arm positions. If you can't hold them all at first, rest and loosely shake your hands and arms in between positions to relax them.

Stand straight, with your feet shoulder-width apart, arms hanging loosely by your sides, knees slightly bent. If you're sitting down uncross your legs and let your arms hang as loosely as possible. Relax your body and throat, and breathe in. As you do the following movements, feel the sound and colour pouring from your fingertips like laser beams. We'll begin by focusing on the root chakra at the base of the spine, breathing in a vibrant red colour.

Moving Sounds: Chakra Chart

Sound	Colour	Chakra	Arm Movement	
I am	white	whole body	arms extended either side like cross	
ooh	purple	crown	arms straight up towards sky	
ohm	indigo	third eye	fingers touching above head to form pyramid	
ee	blue	throat	arms shoulder height, elbows at rectangles, palms facing in	
oh	green	heart	arms make circle above head, fingers touching	
or	yellow	solar plexus	arms extended straight out at shoulder level	
ay	orange	sacral	arms pointed towards ground at diagonal slant	
ah	red	root	extend arms towards ground, swing backwards and forwards	

Ah: Breathe in the colour red to the root and exhale with the sound *ah*, swinging your arms backwards and forwards for a slow eight counts. Repeat three times.

Ay: Now breathe in again through the nose, pulling the energy up from the root to the sacral chakra with the colour orange. Point your arms diagonally towards the earth. Breathe in orange to the sacral chakra, and exhale with the sound *ay* for a slow eight counts. Repeat three times.

Or: Now breathe the energy up from the navel to the solar

plexus, with the colour yellow. Extend both arms straight out at shoulder level. Feel the energy coming out of your fingers. Breathe in yellow to the solar plexus and exhale with the sound *or* for a slow eight counts. Repeat three times.

Oh: Breathe in once more, this time moving the energy up from the solar plexus to the heart centre, with the colour green. Raise your arms to form a circle above your head, fingertips touching, and send the sound *oh* out from your heart. Breathe in green to the heart and exhale with the sound *oh* for a slow eight counts. Repeat three times.

Ee: Now breathe the energy up from the heart to the throat centre with the colour blue. Your arms should be at shoulder height, elbows bent, palms facing in. Breathe in blue to the throat, and exhale with the sound *ee* for a slow eight counts. Repeat three times.

Ohm: Breathe the energy up from the throat to the third eye centre on the forehead, with the colour indigo. Arms still at shoulder height, touch your fingers above the head to form a pyramid shape. Breathe in indigo to the third eye, and exhale with the sound *ohm* for a slow eight counts. Repeat three times.

Ooh: Now breathe the energy up from the third eye to the crown with the colour purple, arms extended straight up towards the sky. Breathe in purple to the crown, and exhale with the sound *ooh* for a slow eight counts. Repeat three times.

I am: Finally, breathe pure white light in through your whole body and extend your arms fully to right and left, like a cross, as every cell of your being affirms *I am*. Breathe in white through the whole body, and exhale with the sound *I am* for a slow eight counts. Repeat three times.

Relax your arms and allow the energy to circulate through you. Stand or sit with your eyes closed and experience what it's like to be your real self, in every cell of your body. Feel the vibrancy. Sound yourself alive!

Partners in Sound

You will by now be starting to feel the energy vibrating from your palms and fingertips when you are using sound. It's also a good learning experience to get feedback from somebody else, and Moving Sounds is a great way to do this with a partner.

Moving sounds with partners

Ask your partner to stand straight, with feet shoulder-width apart, knees slightly bent, arms hanging loosely by their sides, eyes closed. If they're sitting down, they should ideally be sideways on an upright chair to give you access to either side of the body. Otherwise work with both hands directed towards the front of the body.

Stand at right-angles to your partner so you are facing their side. Place one hand in front of the body and one hand behind, but don't touch them. Move your hands in and out towards the body to see if you can feel their aura. This is the energy field surrounding each person and it varies individually. If the aura is small, you will feel able to move your hands close in to the body. If it is large, your hands will stay further away. Once you have gauged the size of the aura, keep your hands at this distance for the whole exercise.

Now bend your knees slightly, keeping your back straight, to align your hands either side of your partner's root chakra. All your partner has to do is stand quietly and enjoy the experience; but if they want, they can also make the sounds with you, slowly breathing their energy up to the crown.

Ah: Visualize a vibrant red colour pouring from your hands and fingertips and filling the whole of your partner's base chakra with life and vitality. Breathe in the colour red, and exhale with the sound *ah* for a slow eight counts. Repeat three times.

Ay: Breathe in again through the nose and pull the energy up by moving your hands from the root to the sacral chakra. Breathe in the colour orange and exhale with the sound *ay* for a slow eight counts. Repeat three times.

Or: Breathe in again and pull the energy up by moving your hands from the navel to the solar plexus, feeling a warm golden yellow emanating from them. Breathe in the colour yellow and exhale with the sound *or* for a slow eight counts. Repeat three times.

Oh: Breathe in once more, this time drawing the energy up as you move your hands from the solar plexus to the heart centre, sending out a healing, harmonious green. Breathe in the colour green and exhale with the sound *oh* for a slow eight counts. Repeat three times.

Ee: Now pull the energy up from the heart by moving your hands to the throat centre, sending out a crystal clear blue. Breathe in the colour blue and exhale with the sound *ee* for a slow eight counts. Repeat three times.

Ohm: Now we're going to move the energy up with our hands from the throat to the third eye on the forehead, the centre of wisdom, with a deep blue indigo. Breathe in the colour indigo and exhale with the sound *ohm* for a slow eight counts. Repeat three times.

Ooh: Now reach up and place both hands directly above your partner's head, pulling the energy up from the third eye to the crown, and visualize a beautiful violet purple streaming from your hands. Breathe in the colour purple and exhale with the sound *ooh* for a slow eight counts. Repeat three times.

I am: Finally, use your intuition and allow your hands to go to any area on your partner's body that you feel needs healing and love, emanating pure white light from your hands. Breathe in pure white energy through your whole body, and exhale with the sound *I am* for a slow eight counts. Repeat three times.

Continue to sing *I am* and visualize the energy circulating through your partner. See the cells of their body like perfect white crystalline structures, singing with joy. Take five or ten minutes' rest to discuss with your partner what you both experienced. If your partner is willing, perhaps you can swop roles and allow them to try the sounds on you, even if they're not used to working with sound. It's good to be on the receiving end and you will always learn from it in some way.

Self-healing Sounds

I spoke earlier about using the individual sounds on yourself, and you can develop this further by 'tuning in' to parts of your body which you know have problems, finding a sound that feels good, and sending it for as long as you like. Direct the sound with your hands and add whatever colour comes to mind. Sending pure sound into those areas which have become 'out of tune' will reawaken the cellular memory of what the perfect, original sound was.

Someone once brought their elderly mother with them to a workshop. She had never been to one before and was quite shocked to feel the energy tingling in her hands. At home the next day she experimented on her aches and pains. To her delight, she discovered that the sound of her own voice really helped. We all have so much at our fingertips without realizing it – and the bonus with sound is that it has no side-effects!

If you use sound to release lumps and knots in your body, don't be surprised if an old feeling or emotional memory reappears. We lock away so many painful secrets and constant repetitive negative thoughts about a particular situation seem to form a clump. When I used sound on a small cyst in myself, I was intrigued after five minutes to re-experience emotions which I'd buried at the age of nineteen during a traumatic situation; which leads me rather neatly to the next subject.

Releasing Emotional Patterns

In the Introduction I described how I discovered how to release emotional patterning trapped in the body. I continue to use the process to this day. It is extremely useful, simple and not dangerous in any way.

What I realized is that any situation which is unreasonably upsetting us in the present moment relates, nine times out of ten, to a programme created by trauma in early childhood (usually the first four years). By the time we reach adulthood, we are carrying around inside us the cellular memory of situations which are no longer appropriate to us, and the energy of which we no longer need in our lives. We draw to us new situations and people who will mirror the original traumatic emotion in order for us to heal and release it now.

CASE STUDY: Sexual Abuse Released

Alison was a married woman in her fifties with children. With soft features and short-cropped hair, she was neatly dressed almost to the point of severity in a masculine-style trouser suit. We talked briefly, and I found her to be a gentle spirit who felt over-burdened by the demands of her family. In particular she wanted to rebuild a closer relationship with her husband.

I began the sound session as usual with a peaceful guided meditation, but was totally unprepared for her reaction. As soon as I began to tone, Alison opened her mouth and let out a scream of rage which continued at full volume for the next half-hour. I was sitting at her head when it happened, and moved quickly to check the energy centres. As soon as I placed my hands over the root chakra, the words 'sexual abuse' came into my mind. The whole centre vibrated with it and mentally I saw a picture of an old man standing over a cot with a small child in it. Alison's screams continued, interspersed by strange, almost inhuman sounds which seemed to express deep disgust.

As I continued to clear her body with sound, her intake of breath between the screams became so sharp I was afraid she would hyperventilate. I knew I had to make a decision: was my intuition correct, or should I stop the session and get help? Again and again, I checked her root chakra. Still it said 'sexual abuse', still the screams continued, so I ceased toning and placed both hands on her solar plexus. As she inhaled I pushed gently down, telling her to breathe into my hands. Slowly, the screaming subsided and she became calm. I used gentle sounds to heal and soothe her, telling her she was safe and nothing could harm her.

We talked at length after the session, and she said a feeling had risen voluntarily in her as though she was going to be sick. It was exactly as I had seen. The sound had unlocked a cellular memory she'd hidden away as a child, and the full horror had returned of her grandfather lifting the cot sheets and abusing her. The helplessness of the child, the fear and the anger had all burst from her in a violent explosion, and now she felt a huge sense of relief and gratefulness to have released it. We did some work on forgiveness, and she told me that, although she was married, she had never felt relaxed with men in her entire life, particularly during sexual inter-course. She had always felt there was a barrier, but never understood why or what.

Over the next few months we worked together and slowly Alison began to express her real woman. She had always been afraid to display her femininity and it was lovely to see her hairstyle and clothes change. She began to put the fun back into her sex life with massage oils and pretty underwear, and said her feelings during sex had become much deeper and more beautiful. The block she had experienced with men in general was dissolving. She didn't feel so nervous any more in their company. In fact, she felt almost 'reborn'.

Our greatest asset in childhood is also our weakest point. A child intuitively knows the truth of what is taking place around it. Parents and adults appear god-like and, even when they behave destructively, the child still instinctively believes the adults are in the right and automatically takes the blame when things go wrong. How many of us thought it was our fault when our parents argued, or split up, and took on their responsibility for healing their relationship?

Children are also perfect sponges for picking up learned behaviour patterns; this can even begin in the womb, when repetitive thoughts and worries can become imprinted. Have you ever experienced a recurring feeling that doesn't belong to you, or make any sense? One woman could not understand why a strange thought of 'There's no point, because it will never work out' kept flooding through her mind. It was not something she believed. Eventually she managed to release it. It had been triggered by her mother's feelings, ingested with every piece of chocolate she ate during pregnancy. Her mother's experience (and thus belief) was that men were able to get what they wanted from life, but women were not. Consequently, the mother killed her hopes and dreams dead with the repeated thought that they could never be realized for her, so there was no point in trying. This idea was neatly passed on to the baby in her womb.

Releasing your own problems

The technique of release is simple. Sit comfortably in a quiet place where you will not be disturbed. Have at hand a box of tissues and a pillow. Close your eyes and bring into your mind the situation or person currently causing you distress. Really imagine it as though it were happening now – see the faces, hear the conversations, the tone of voice, the criticisms and accusations. Re-create it as vividly as if you were in the centre of it again, and allow yourself totally to experience the feelings in your body, so that your heart may even start beating faster from adrenalin, your stomach may feel sick and your solar plexus full of butterflies.

Pull a sound out of the air and begin to repeat it, over and over. If you want to go higher, or lower, do so, until you have found a sound that begins to really resonate with you. Holding the situation in your mind's eye and your body, keep making the sound and breathing as deeply as you can until you experience a sudden flash of connection, as though a light has suddenly switched on inside you and you trigger backwards to the situation which upset you in the first place. It may take time.

You'll feel a great rush of feeling inside. If you are releasing anger, scream, yell, even pound the pillow with your fists as though it were the person you were angry with. You may find you begin by yelling at one person who suddenly becomes your mother or father. If you are releasing grief, clutch the pillow to your solar plexus, rock back and forth and allow yourself to cry it all out.

When you feel you have expressed everything, use a calming, loving sound to heal that hurt place inside. I also like to write out an affirmation, which can be sung as a positive mantra for a few days. If, for instance, you released a pattern where you felt rejected and criticized, your affirmation could be: 'I am worthy to be loved and supported on all levels.' Or if your self-confidence was destroyed in some way, you could affirm: 'I am an amazing being with unique talents to give to the world!'

When you use sound in this way, the layers will peel away like an onion and you will begin to feel freer to express your real self. You will also become more aware of patterns which need releasing as they bubble to the surface. You'll learn to recognize them by vague feelings of uneasiness or depression manifesting for no apparent reason. When you experience all or any of these symptoms, use sound to clear them. You will be surprised at what emerges.

Helping a partner

This technique also works well with a partner. Help them release by sitting opposite them, holding their hands as they go through the process, sounding the sound with them, and even comforting them in your arms afterwards. I would advise you not to use this mode of releasing with couples in workshops unless you can be sure of a very supportive environment, because it is very powerful and people need total freedom to express everything they are feeling. Also an entire workshop simultaneously processing deeply buried emotions could become a nightmare!

Sound Relationships

Ever had that feeling that you'd like to wipe the slate clean, and start all over again with your relationships? Sometimes a breakdown can become a breakthrough, as we look back and see a long line of people who neatly fitted into a pattern we'd created. Now the pattern no longer exists – but what about the debris we left behind? Here is a simple, effective way of clearing the energy created by your relationships with men, women, family and work colleagues.

Sit quietly and tune yourself in with the chakra sound meditation from root to crown, ending by bringing the energy back to your heart with the sound *oh* and colour green. Imagine you are breathing sound and colour in and out through your heart centre. Now see the group you want to clear standing in a line in front of you, one behind the other. For instance, if you want to heal and clear love relationships, the first in the 'queue' will be your latest, behind them the one before and so on, stretching right back to the first relationship you can remember. If you're dealing with family or colleagues, put the person you are closest to at the head of the queue and the rest behind in descending order of importance. Alternatively, just allow people to present themselves in your mind's eye in order of who you have the most to clear with.

Try to envisage the queue standing so that their heart chakras are in line with one another. Summon the Angels of Sound: ask one to stand behind you and another to stand behind the last person in the queue. Now begin to sound an *oh*, sending the energy from your heart with a pure green light through the heart chakra of the first person. See the sound and colour linking your hearts, clearing and healing all pain and problems from the past. Continue with the sound and envisage it coming out of that person's back and into the heart of the next in line. You may discover to your surprise that you have access to people's feelings and motivations, which will help you to understand their behaviour. You may also feel resistance from people to move through their hearts and you may feel their problems. If this happens, speak to their higher self (the part which knows the truth and is not controlled by the ego/personality), asking to be allowed to clear the past and to be protected from the present in the spirit of love.

Work through the whole queue in this way, repeating the healing process until all blocks are removed and you can effortlessly send sound and colour from your heart through every single heart in the line, and out the other end to the angel.

Now change the sound from *oh* to *ooh*, transforming the green to vibrant gold. Strongly emit this new sound and colour from your heart, this time sending it into the first person to energize and empower them. Continue the process down the line, until you can once more send sound and colour right the way through and out the other end to the angel.

Now continue to tone and envisage the golden energy you sent out returning to you, like a beam of solid gold light directed back into your heart from the hearts of everyone in the queue. Allow your heart to receive fully, visualizing it expanding and relaxing and bathing in the pure gold. Feel the energy pouring right through you and coming out of the back of your heart chakra into the angel behind you. Know that the wounds of the past are healed, and experience what it feels like to be acknowledged, loved and supported for who you truly are. Continue with the sound until you feel a sense of oneness between you and every person in the line. See the sound and colour emanating from the two angels to form a circle of light around everyone involved.

Now let everyone file past you, one by one. As they leave the circle, look into their eyes, bless them, and thank them for the many gifts they gave you with the lessons you learned through being together. Continue to tone for a few more minutes, and really have a sense of your own 'solid gold' individuality and beauty. See your own golden aura which will now attract to you new attitudes from old relationships, and new relationships born from the new you. Seal this energy around you like a golden halo, empowering and filling it with the sound. When you are ready, thank the Angels of Sound, open your eyes – and smile with the joy of being alive!

Sounding Out the Ancestors

Not only do we carry programming from our lives in the cells of our body, but very often we're holding ancestral patterns which have been subconsciously passed down the generations. You may find you become the healing nucleus for your family in that as you consciously release and change, they too begin to open and alter. You can use the method described in the previous section to heal your family line, visualizing your ancestors stretching before you and sending the sound through them to clear all negativity, and allowing them to empower you with all their positive attributes. End by thanking the past generations for all they have given you with the gift of your life.

Sending Out Sounds

I remember once desperately wanting to speak to a friend of mine in Australia. He was flourishing financially and I was struggling. I couldn't pay for a phone call so I decided to send him a 'sound message'. I held a clear picture of him in my mind and began to emit a loving sound, visualizing it coming out of my heart in one long continuous wave going all the way to Australia. Within a few hours, he phoned me!

It doesn't always work like that, but you can send sound to people in the form of messages, love and healing. Just hold that person in your mind's eye and your heart, choose an appropriate sound and colour and begin to sing, directing it either to the part of them that needs healing or straight into their heart. Use your hands as well, if you want to. Imagine the person is standing in front of you and place your hands exactly where you feel they can do the most good. Ask the Angels of Sound to transport your love to the person in question, and see the sound issuing forth from your mouth like coloured streamers whose energy keeps going in a straight line until it lovingly reaches its destination.

Soundless Sound

Do everything as described above, but sound the sound inside you so that you only hear its pitch and tone in your head. Then send it silently. This method is very useful in public situations, when people are panicking or in crisis, and when working with chronically ill patients who might find the actual sung tones too strong for their system.

Soundless sound is also wonderful to incorporate when you are giving a massage, particularly when working on the sensitive areas of the face. As you massage, intuit the relevant tone and sound it in your head, sending it into the body tissues to cleanse, purify and energize. Use this soundless sound on any areas of the body where you feel there is pain, blockage or disharmony.

Sound Asleep

For best results lie on your back so you can breathe deeply; but if you can't manage this just try and relax your body, whatever position it's in. Focus on the breath as usual, breathing in through the nose to the sacral chakra, imagining that channel of air which ends just below the navel. Allow yourself a few breaths and settle down into a slow rhythm. Then, as you exhale through the nose, silently sound a long *ooh* (or whatever sound suits you) in your mind: that is, breathe in to the sacral chakra, breathe out to the silent sound *ooh*. Continue to do this, allowing the *ooh* to get longer and longer, and your breathing slower and slower until you fall asleep.

Peaceful Sounds

In Chapter 3, I mentioned the Angels of Dissonance, who work to create discord and disharmony from the vibrations of pure sound. Our modern world is polluted with noise and you may find when you begin your sound work that a loud, disturbing noise appears and distracts you.

One day when I was trying to meditate with all sorts of cacophony going on around me, I realized that if the Angels of Dissonance really were trying to disturb me there was one way I could stop them. I walked around the entire flat sounding the purest tones I could muster in every room, sending the sound high into the ceiling, down into every corner, along the corridors and out through the doors and windows. The noise above me stopped and there was absolute silence for the rest of the day. This method also works with noisy neighbours.

I've also noticed that, when I've begun a sound session in someone's flat and loud music is vibrating the floor above or below, after a few minutes the music magically stops and I am allowed to proceed in peace. There is nothing more powerful than the pure sound of love, used in compassionate service.

Heavy Metal Sounds

In the seventies, I suffered a great deal from tinnitis (high-pitched ringing tones in the ears) which caused by performing on stage with rock bands where we used thousands of watts of sound amplification to produce extremes of volume. There is still some controversy about the long-term effects of exposure to high volumes of music but, currently, there is no scientific evidence that rock music is damaging to normal ears. I discovered that the ear has a mechanism which is activated by extremes of volume and functions like a 'noise gate', shutting off to limit sound levels and protect the inner ear. Temporary deafness disappears as the ear returns to normal, but if you are constantly exposed to loud noise, this sound limiting device remains in place for longer and longer periods and so it takes longer for your hearing to recover.

It is true that different frequencies of music affect different energy centres of the body, and the throbbing bass end of rock music clearly vibrates the root chakra and basic life-force energy. Teenagers going through puberty into adolescence have little idea of what to do with their own life-force energy surging through their bodies, and for most of them heavy metal music is a means of expressing themselves and rebelling against authority. If children are grounded and supported with enough love, they will take what is good and fun and energizing from the music and walk away from any drugs, alcohol and the need to lose themselves in the extremes of head-banging, numbing volume and the occasional negative lyrics that heavy metal seems to inspire.

Grounding the Sound

When you start to work extensively with sound healing, you may find you get very light-headed. You can ground yourself with a glass of water, or use a visualization to bring you back to earth. The best one I know is to 'grow' a tail which gradually extends from your coccyx and roots right into the earth. See the layers of the earth as the tail extends deeper and deeper, and really feel yourself anchored to that lovely, rich, earthy energy. When you feel grounded, you can slowly pull up the tail and pack it away again, ready for the next time.

Closing Down

We've been working with sound to open ourselves up and clear out old energies. But we also need to protect this new openness, and there are a number of ways we can close down if we need to. At the end of your sound session, go through your chakras one by one, seeing them as beautiful lotuses, and close the petals tight, sealing them with a blessing (see below). Or you can place one angel in front of you, one behind, and one either side as guardians of your own sacred space. Most often, I simply surround myself with a circle of gold light, like a big positive bubble, and see myself held safely inside. You will soon learn to know which chakra is feeling 'invaded' by someone's energy, and quickly protect it.

Focus Work

Are you feeling brave? If you haven't already tried the technique of releasing an emotional pattern, now's the time! Follow the instructions and let the sound do its work. Don't forget to write your affirmation afterwards.

When you've completed your release, slowly go through the process of closing down. Sit quietly and follow your breathing in through your nose, down to the sacral chakra. Breathe in the gold light. Now, focusing on your root chakra, see a beautiful red lotus there and slowly close the petals. At the sacral chakra, close an orange lotus. At the solar plexus, a yellow one. At the heart, a green one. At the throat, a blue one. At the third eye, an indigo one. At the crown, a purple one. Imagine a circle of pure gold surrounding you, vibrating light and sound. Hear the voices of the angels as they fill this circle with beautiful tones. Breathe that feeling of being safe, protected and honoured for who you truly are right into the cells of your body. Know to your innermost core that you will effortlessly attract to you all that vibrates at the same positive frequency of love and light. Experience the true lightness of being held, supported and abundantly loved.

Chapter 5

I AM A TRANSMITTER: USING SOUND ON OTHERS

From my experiences over the years as a sound healer I've developed a system of working on patients which is simple, practical and effective, based on the sounds and colours linked to the chakras. I find in healing that whether the symptoms are emotional, mental, spiritual or physical, the way to clear them initially is to unblock the chakras. Once energy can circulate freely it affects the whole body, and with regular sound sessions you can begin to get to the root of the problem.

But bear in mind that what I describe in the following pages is merely a structure for you to work from. Take from it what you find useful, and discover your own techniques to complement it. Sound healing is a continuing adventure, and once you begin to work with it something new and amazing will appear with each session.

Remember you will be slowly removing layers as you tune your patients back into health, so be aware of the many different levels you are working on. In one session you could be healing the physical body, in the next focusing on the emotional, in the next on the mental or the spiritual, and finally on the etheric. Or sometimes it may be a mixture of them all. Gradually, you will learn to differentiate and create the harmony and balance your patient needs to be truly sound in body and mind.

Prayer and Ritual

As described in Chapter 3, you will have your mattress or massage table ready, a blanket for warmth, a box of tissues for the patient, a glass of water, a fresh flower and a candle to light. Before the patient arrives, warm your voice up with some of the exercises described earlier, then sit in meditation for a few minutes. Sound an octave of sound (the eight notes from a low *doh* to the next highest *doh*), intuitively choosing a pitch to start at and a sound to use. Use this octave to tune in to your higher self, because the sum of your attunement and energy will affect the sound quality when you begin to sing.

I always ask the patient what they want from the healing session. Many people feel they are not allowed to ask for what they want, let alone to receive it! I always emphasize that this healing time is specifically for them – no requests are allowed for anyone else – and, once they have focused on what they need, I take their hands and make a prayer, asking to be a channel for their healing angel to sing through.

I then light the candle with another prayer to call in the Christ light and clear any dark energy from the room, asking that I may be linked to the Angels of Sound. When I feel this connection, I thank them and am ready to proceed.

The longer I work with sound and the clearer I become on all body levels, the stronger is my connection with the angels. I hear them speak to me, and on the odd occasion I have been told off for the state of my physical body. I was once called in to do an impromptu sound session after eating a lot of cheese the night before. The message came through quite sharply that 'the vessel [me] must be absolutely clear in future to access the highest rays of healing, because the vibrations of animals in the body made it too gross to receive this particular energy'. Another time I really was denied access because I had drunk three glasses of wine the night before. This didn't mean I couldn't work – I just couldn't work from such a high place, so unfortunately the quality of the healing I gave was limited. I learned from those experiences to be prepared at all times!

A Guided Meditation to Relax

I always begin and end my sessions at the head, the perfect place to tune into the whole body with a guided relaxation. Some people are very nervous so the more you can calm someone, the greater will be the benefit of the sound.

I usually begin by asking the patient to breathe in through the 'channel of air' to the sacral chakra, and then to imagine gold or white light pouring in through the crown. Next, I talk my way slowly through the entire body, telling them to visualize the light flowing into each point, relaxing, calming and soothing them. By the end I am in tune with every part of that person's body, and feel totally linked to them; my own body is also relaxed.

Again, what you develop for your initial relaxation technique is entirely up to you. Learn how to use your speaking voice to great effect with key phrases like 'sinking deeper and deeper' and 'here you can totally let go'. It is vital to help your patient experience a 'safe space' where problems and fears are left behind and they can allow themselves to be healed.

Once I've relaxed the patient with a guided meditation, I take them on a 'journey' which ends by placing them in a pool of healing water and calling their angel to them. Usually I ask people to go back to childhood and visualize themselves standing in a garden they remember, because for most of us childhood was a time when we had tons of energy, very little wrong with our bodies, and a fun approach to life. The key phrases here are 'an adventure about to be experienced' or 'a journey to be undertaken', and 'a healing to be received'. The visualization continues with the child leaving the garden to follow a path through nature, encountering sun, wind, water and wood on the way. The final destination, the pool of healing water, provides a sense of returning to the warmth, comfort and support of the womb.

By this time your patient should either be asleep or in a state of deep relaxation, and you are ready to begin. Call their angel, and ask them to see the angel in their mind's eye standing by the pool. You too may see the angel. Sometimes they are archetypals dressed in white, and at other times they are quite extraordinary, with vivid rainbow colours.

Some people find it extremely moving to experience their own angel for the first time, because they have never felt such love and support before. Often, they cry. You can explain to your patient that their angel was with them not only before they were born but also at the time of their birth, and has been beside them at every moment of their life. Their angel will also be there when they pass over into the other worlds. I always tell people that when they look and see how beautiful their angel is, they are only seeing a mirror image of themselves in their highest form of pure compassion. The truth is that your own personal angel loves you more than love itself, and is there to help reflect back to you your own inner beauty.

I end the guided journey in the pool with the words, 'And so the angel begins to sing.' At that point I silently ask the angel to sing through me, open my mouth and intuitively emit a sound.

How Will the Patient React?

The most common reaction is to fall into a deep sleep or state of extreme relaxation. Even if the patient is asleep the sound will be just as effective.

However, when some patients release parts of their body vibrate, shake or tremble uncontrollably, while other people cry. One woman I was working on went back to a child abuse situation she'd blocked for her entire life, and screamed with anger for twenty minutes. I continued to tone, placed my hands on her solar plexus and asked her to breathe into them. Eventually she became as peaceful and reborn as a new lamb.

This latter kind of release is rare. As they become mesmerized by the sound of your voice, most people will simply drift away and have a very pleasant experience. One strange phenomenon that patients report is that, once you begin the sound and are moving around the body, they can't tell exactly where you are. Someone said it's as though the sound fills their entire body and that is all they are aware of.

Sounding the Sound

Begin at the head

The simplest way to discover the best sound for a particular person is to sound an octave of the musical scale. So pick any note but don't make it a high one, as you are going to go up the scale, very slowly, note by note, choosing a vowel sound and sounding the tones. As you do this, try and feel which note vibrates well with the body you're working on. You'll soon discover that a particular vowel sound and pitch feel really good. When you've completed your octave, come back to this note and keep sounding it.

Remember that the head, where you are starting, is a particularly sensitive part of the body. You must constantly monitor your patient's reactions, and if there are signs of discomfort lower your volume and pitch immediately. You'll soon learn to recognize the difference between somebody releasing with the sound, and expressing any pain from it – although, I have to say, the latter rarely happens.

I will mention here again that you must never use loud, high-pitched sound on a chronically ill person, particularly if they have cancer. Sound can help, but make it gentle, warm, loving and soft, and only go up the octave to the mid-tones. If the patient gets stronger, you can go higher. But remember that people with severe illness can actually be damaged by loud, high tones. If you're at all unsure, place your hands intuitively in the right position and tone the notes silently inside you.

Once I have found an appropriate tone and pitch I usually sit at the head of my patient for five to ten minutes, sounding that particular sound. This simultaneously mesmerizes them and balances the two sides of your brain as you work, allowing your intuition to flow. When you become more practised, pictures will start appearing in your mind and words will float into your consciousness. You'll begin to pick up the patterns vibrating in the body you're working on, and you may even become aware of some of the root causes of their patterning from childhood.

Stay at the head as long as you like, sounding sound. Use your intuition about when to change the sound, to what and for how long. After a while you may become aware of thoughts and words programmed into someone (usually by their parents) which may have caused them to have little self-worth and self-respect. Start clearing these. The words spoken to us and about us when we are young affect the way we see ourselves, speak about ourselves and hear ourselves in later life, so as I make the sound I often 'pull' great yarns of negative patterning out of someone's brain, ears, eyes and mouth.

Work for as long as you deem necessary, with as many different sounds as you like, to clear all aspects of the head area. Allow your hands to move freely. Sometimes I point mine in the shape of an arrowhead, to direct the sound, or create intricate patterns in the air as I tone. On other occasions, it's almost as if my hands have a mind of their own and make ritual movements without any input from me.

Moving through the chakras

When you feel you've accomplished all you can at the head, move to the side of the body to begin working one by one on the chakras, starting as usual at the root with the sound *ah*. Once again, choose any pitch you want, although it is always better to start with lower notes at the root and move up the body with higher notes. Work with *ah* to begin with, clearing the chakra, and envisaging it opening to allow the energy to run freely. If you want to change to another sound, do; but it is important to start work on each chakra with the correct sound, and then change.

Once you feel you have cleared the root, move up to the sacral with the sound *ay*, the solar plexus with *or*, the heart with *oh*, the throat with *ee*, the third eye with *ohm*, until you reach the crown again with *ooh*, by which time you should be able to sweep your hand up the chakras from root to crown, clearing and pulling the energy up. You can also use the relevant chakra colours, intuiting if somebody has too much of one colour or too little, and sending it in or drawing it out with the sound you make.

Crystals

We touched upon crystals in Chapter 3. See p. 44 for how to tune crystals to an octave, create a healing crystal circle to place someone inside, and tune a crystal with a patient's personal mantra or specific tones.

I don't work with crystals, but if you are drawn to them you can hold them in one hand and point them at the chakra or part of the body you're clearing, imagining purifying energy pouring out of the crystal as you emit the sound. Crystals can also be used to energize by beaming energy from yourself via the crystal into a particular area.

Laser Sound Operations

After working with sound for some time, I began to purify the tones by changing the shape of my mouth and lips. It felt as though the sound was becoming focused into a pinpoint beam of energy, and as I toned I could feel this energy streaming from the tips of my fingers as well.

Then something else began to happen. As I was clearing people's chakras, I became aware in my mind's eye of all sorts of strange objects blocking them, in particular clumps of negative thoughts and feelings which had piled up and were clogging the body. I began to use the sound like a laser ray, as though I was surgically removing things.

Once I became accustomed to this 'laser surgery', a whole new world opened up for me. There were stones of sadness, black balls of fear, jagged crystals of pain, swords of anger and chains of control to be removed. I saw that we not only take on other people's patterns and truths, but weave around ourselves an invisible suit of clothing fashioned from our words and thoughts. With one patient this 'armour' had become so solid that I felt I was using sound like a welder's torch to split it open and enable the real person to emerge. In the main we create these shields as protection: but sometimes we unconsciously continue the process to such an extent that what began as a shield from pain becomes an impenetrable wall that nothing can pierce – including joy and love.

CASE STUDY: A Young Man with an Angry Father

Alex was in his mid-twenties, tall, slim, agile and intelligent. A farmer's son, he had a natural affinity with animals and the earth. He fearlessly enjoyed the adrenalin rush of hang-gliding and ski-jumping, but emotional feelings jangled loud alarm bells in him.

A vegetarian, he still lived at home but was experiencing problems with his father, not wishing to follow in his footsteps as a cattle farmer. His father had a strong and overpowering personality, and the intense anger between the two had become so strong that Alex avoided him out of fear. They had not spoken for some time, which only made matters worse. Alex felt depressed and powerless in the situation.

During the sound session, I focused on Alex's solar plexus. I became aware of his habit of negating his thoughts and ideas before he'd even fully given them birth, and the energy centre was packed solid with every time he'd said 'No' to himself and destroyed a thought by not expressing it. He was obviously a wonderfully creative person, but was killing off his ideas with the belief that there was no point in even trying.

I used sound to 'cut a hole' in the solar plexus and began to remove the solid mass of negativity. Alex said afterwards he was nearly sick at this point. I then 'healed' the remaining wound with sound and filled it with positive energy. At the end of the session we worked with sound and visualization to cut the ties with Alex's father, to empower Alex and to ask that he be given the space and courage to express his own ideas.

When I spoke with him afterwards, he confirmed he had given up all hope and repressed his own creativity, as he could not see any way out of the situation. He said he felt lighter and less afraid, and a few days later phoned to tell me the sound healing had really made a difference: he had found the courage to face his father, realizing that all he had to do was stand his ground like a man and answer back. He no longer felt afraid and his father, sensing that, had changed his attitude.

As always, if you want to change a situation on the outside, change the inside of you first!

The Angels of Sound are invaluable assistants in all these 'operations', handing me what I feel I need in that moment (such as a tap to attach to a particular chakra to drain the tears trapped there), and taking from me any strange objects I remove. These objects are usually visual manifestations of states of energy that exist in the emotional, mental and spiritual bodies. They may not yet have reached the physical plane, so it is vital to clear them.

Another way I use laser sound is by 'drilling holes' in the crown to let the positive energy in or pull the negative energy out – a kind of sonic trepanning. Sound can also be sent from the other end of the body via the feet, up the backbone to the crown. More of that later.

Clearing the Body

Once you've worked on the chakras, opening and toning them as much as you can, intuitively find a sound to clear the whole body one half at a time, trawling with your hands in an upward movement. Start at the foot, moving up one leg and one half of the torso to the shoulder, then down the arm, sweeping everything out through the hand. If you feel drawn to a particular area of the body, sensing energy blocks or physical problems, find an appropriate sound and keep working for as long as you like. The only time limit is your stamina to keep toning.

Feet: Sound Reflexology

Once you've finished with the torso move down to the feet. Usually at this point, I drop pitch so the sounds become lower. I love working on the feet. You can learn so much from them. Every callous and bunion tells a story – usually of overbearing siblings and controlling parents trying to manipulate or force someone into their way of being. Sound can help to release the painful memories and you can extract the negative energy through the soles. Just imagine there's a tiny thread of it sticking out and begin to reel it in like a fishing line. I often feel as though I'm pulling out long streams of thoughts which other people

Reflexology Chart

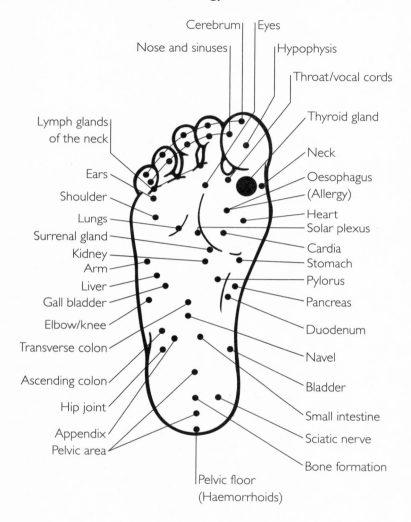

have programmed into my patient. Be careful as you work to pull the 'thread' to one side of you and not directly into you so you can hand it over to the angels behind to dispose of.

In some instances, I've used the feet for anchoring. When I was working on a woman in the early stages of multiple sclerosis, it felt as though her spirit was not in her body, but hovering above. Using sound, I called the spirit in, pulled it down to the feet, and rather like Peter Pan and his shadow, tied it in knots under the soles to keep it there!

This may all sound highly unlikely, but remember we are working on many different planes with many different energies. Whatever you do will have a positive effect, however odd it may seem to the logical brain.

As anyone who has experienced reflexology knows, the nerve endings in the soles of our feet correspond to different organs in the body. The reflexology diagram shows you which areas of the body relate to which point on the foot. All you need to do is focus the sound with your fingers and voice. Once when working on a chronic fatigue syndrome patient who had subconsciously closed down whole areas of her body through intense fear, I became aware that I could use sound on her feet to relink the heart energy back to the rest of her body.

Another foot-oriented therapy, the metamorphic technique of healing, also links the inner edge of the foot to the spinal cord (the big toe end representing the crown and the heel end representing the coccyx, with the months of gestation in the womb when the foetus was formed in between the two). Sound works really well in relation to the actual skeletal structure, so it's always beneficial to use it in these areas when someone has back problems.

Energizing the Body

Once you've finished working on the feet you can return to the chakras again, this time to energize them with sound. Start at the root chakra (*ah* and colour red), focusing on pouring strong, vibrant life force energy into it, and move up to the sacral (*ay* and orange), filling it with joy and expectancy. Next, send unlimited self-confidence to the solar plexus (*or* and yellow), harmony to the heart (*oh* and green), clear, truthful communication to the throat (*ee* and blue), empowerment of wisdom and intuition into the third eye (*ohm* and indigo), finishing at the crown (*ooh* and purple) with universal love.

These are the basic energies behind the sounds and colours. While you've been working on someone's body, you will probably have tuned into some of the patterns and fears inherent in them, so what I have written above is only a guideline for you to work from. You will come to know what is required where, and sometimes it is even useful to link one chakra to the other in an arc of your hand. I often join the solar plexus to the throat in this way, when someone lacks the courage to speak their own truth – I try to add the positive confidence of the solar plexus to the throat to empower it. Sometimes I will link the third eye to another chakra where more wisdom is required, or the heart to an area which needs love. I also use the sound *ohm* as a sacred blessing and cleansing for any chakra which has been violated – particularly the root chakra, in instances of sexual abuse.

But once you really start to use these sounds, you will intuitively find your own system and what works best for you.

During this process of energizing the chakras you can also envisage them as beautiful flowers opening; if the chakras have been badly damaged and are not quite ready, plant 'seeds' in them instead. Hold out your hand in expectation, and the angels will give you a seed of joy. 'Plant' it in the relevant chakra and 'water' it with loving sound, so that it may take root. See it sprouting as you tone, and bless it with love. Each time you return to use sound on that person, your compassion will help the seed to transform into a joyful bloom. I particularly like to plant these psychic seeds after removing some of the jagged and cruel obstructions which life has placed in some people's chakras.

Observing Body Language

As you work more with healing, you will find that at a certain point you can go no further without the agreement of the patient. Some people use their illnesses to make themselves interesting, to draw attention to themselves, and to manipulate others. If this sounds unkind, understand that it comes from a place in these people where they believe they are totally unlovable, and can only deserve or attract love and support by being ill in some way. So if they don't feel ready, patients will sometimes use their bodies to block the energy you are sending. You will learn to read the signs, such as crossed legs, hands and arms guarding various parts of the body, heads placed out of alignment with the backbone, and a general disarray of limbs.

But patients will also sometimes give you signs when they have agreed to allow themselves to be healed. There are no hard and fast rules to recognize them, but they are usually linked to balance and alignment. So learn to observe the body language as you are working, keep sounding the notes and praying for compassion, and eventually all will be made clear to you.

Drawing Down the Energy

You've now energized the chakras, so choose a sound and 'trawl' the body again with your hands, allowing yourself to be drawn to wherever energy is needed, and sending it into the system. Stand upright at the feet, at the head or sideways on to the body, or even one after another if you wish. Continue to make your sound, raise your hands diagonally above your head and imagine all the energy from the highest rays of healing pouring from above into your hands and down your arms.

Really allow yourself to experience this feeling as you sing, and when you feel completely charged direct your hands down towards the patient's body, sending all the energy from your fingertips directly into it. If you are standing at the feet, imagine you are pulling the energy from above and directing it into their head, down the backbone to the root and back up again. If you are standing at the head, pull the energy from the root to the crown to the root, and finish with the crown. Continue as long as you like, until you feel your patient is filled with positive energy.

Sealing with Sound

First I like to return to the chakras once more moving from root to crown with sound, weaving and spinning the energy around them by moving my hands together from top to bottom in a figure-of-eight motion. Then, after working on so many different levels and opening up areas possibly closed for years, we need to realign our patient's aura or energy field. I usually 'seal' somebody up with the sound *ooh*, but choose what feels appropriate to you. Sound the tone, stretch your arms out diagonally, with hands pointed, and trace slowly around the edges of the entire body, as though you were painting a line around it with sound. Imagine you are creating a protective seal to hold in the positive vibrations you have made with your toning, and to keep out any negative energy.

Coded Information

Once you have successfully 'sealed' the body, return to the head. Sit at the crown (or stand, if you have been working with a massage table), and finish with as pure a sound as you can make. At this point you can open yourself up as a channel of service to the Angels of Sound, and when this happens you'll be surprised at the beautiful tones which effortlessly pour from your mouth. This is the time when the angels send through any personal information that they have for your patient. I always experience it as a kind of 'coded message' in the tones. All I know is that it is only relevant to the person receiving the healing, and that what they need to know is written within the sound that issues from my mouth.

Coming Back to Earth

A sound session is a journey of discovery for both healer and patient. Once you have sounded your 'coded information', allow your tones to move lower and lower down the musical scale, ending on a low note. Repeat this four or five times.

You now need to bring your patient slowly out of their meditative state. I usually end with the words, 'And the angel stops singing, and says …', because there is always some small message of love and support from their guardian angel. Don't worry if you don't get anything when you first begin: you will eventually.

Next, continue with the guided visualization begun on p. 77 by removing your patient from the pool of healing water, refreshed, relaxed, reborn and revitalized (the words you now use are equally important to imprint a different mind-set in them), and walk them joyfully back on the path to the place where they started their journey. Finish by requesting them to return to the present with all the vital energy and joy of a small child, and impress upon them that the healing they have received will continue over the next few days.

Sound Affirmations

I sometimes find that affirmations come through which are relevant to the healing someone has received during a session. For instance, if they have suffered great loss and pain in their lives, I might intuit, 'I now attract to me all that I need, and my life begins anew.' It's always useful to write these things down for someone. Some affirmations turn themselves into songs, and after a session I'll teach it to the patient for their personal use. Anything you can give someone to sing, chant or affirm to strengthen their own self-worth and courage is a great asset, and if you can provide your patient with 'homework' of this nature it also encourages them to take some responsibility for their own healing in between sessions.

If you have a machine you can record their personal sound, affirmation or chant for them, but remind them to listen to it on speakers, not headphones. For the vibration of the sound to penetrate the body, it must be experienced from outside the auric field. You can also spend a little time after your session or at the next one working with the patient to make sounds with you, and helping them to discover exactly what tones feel good to them.

Sounding Out Past Lives and Passed-over Relationships

I don't intentionally work with past lives, as I find it more relevant to be grounded in the present, and people sometimes like to blame past life relationships for current problems rather than take responsibility for what is happening now. However, on occasions past lives do come through loud and clear.

One woman began to make the sound with me as soon as I began toning, and I was immediately aware that she was very clear in body and spirit. She didn't need healing: the sound session was an empowerment for her. Every note I sang she echoed beautifully with me, even though she was lying down, and her hands simultaneously moved in sacred ritualistic gestures. I saw that she had been a Tibetan Master of Sound in a past life, and that her higher self on a soul level knew exactly what I was doing, without me even speaking a word.

It was a beautiful session. Afterwards, she said she had been unable to stop herself either making the sound or moving her hands, and was shocked when I told her why. She admitted that, whenever she'd been in a church or anywhere that sacred music was being performed, her hands automatically began the ritual gestures. This woman was a perfect example of the notion that we all hold the knowledge within us. I told her she could be a sound healer like me, but that she had the ability to heal the earth as well by chanting at sacred power points.

Past lives may not be the only secrets you become aware of, and when you begin to 'see' things in people you must decide whether or not to tell them. Is the information relevant to what is happening now? Very often it can be helpful, but be aware of the consequences of anything you reveal.

The past can affect us in other ways, too. Many people still in this life have unfinished business with those who have passed over, particularly parents. Just because someone is dead, it doesn't mean their patterns and programming no longer control you. I've had many cases of strong parents literally 'standing over' their grown children and blocking entry, and you would not believe how many mothers have had deep dark secrets which they passed on subconsciously to their daughters to carry for them. Even from the other side, they don't want those secrets to come to light.

If, when you begin your session, you are strongly aware of another presence, work to heal that presence first before you address your patient, because that energy is affecting them. Send your sound to this presence. Ask them what they want, if they are willing to cut the ties and allow the patient to heal, and if you cannot feel any response call in the compassionate Christ light to clear the energy.

CASE STUDY: Past Lives

I believe that too much focus upon past lives can give people an easy escape route for not accepting responsibility for the here and now. However, sometimes, it comes through so strongly I feel I have to mention it, and often it has a relevance to a current state of mind. My feeling is if healing occurs (and it does), the means are less important than the result.

When I began sound on Michael, an upwardly mobile young businessman, the room was filled with Druids in white robes. They clearly told me he had been a Druid in a past life, and was chosen then to receive very special knowledge which he could now use in this incarnation to help the earth. The message was so strong that I felt bound to tell the young man, who already knew he had great power but was not yet ready to harness it in service to the planet.

Another woman, Joanna, had absolutely no fear of death. I saw that in a previous life she had been a priestess on a Pacific island and, out of love for her people, had willingly offered herself as a human sacrifice to enable the crops to grow. Shortly after the sound session she changed both her names and now has the most beautiful lyrical name which means 'gift' – the energy that she brings in this life to all who meet her.

Finally, there was Elizabeth, a beautiful woman who always looked very regal and often dressed in velvet. A sense of hopelessness had dogged her throughout life and left her feeling that there was really no point in trying.

When I began to tone, I saw her as French aristocrat – a worthy woman who did not misuse her position but loved her family and the people working on her estate. When the revolution came, in spite of the regard and equality with which she had treated the local peasants she was pilloried, shamed and taunted until the moment of her death, when she also saw her son beheaded. Thus in this life she could not see the point in doing anything well, because in her previous life she'd done everything right and still been executed.

I worked hard with sound to 'rejoin' her body with her head, and the session completely cleared the woman's underlying feeling of pointlessness. Strangely, many of her friends had often told her it was as though her head was not joined to her body! Several sessions later she has moved house, rebuilt her relationship with her mother, and is striding forward very positively in her life – still graciously dressed in velvet so that, whenever I look at her, I can't help but see the French aristocrat.

Cutting the ties with sound

Paul Solomon always used to say, 'If you love someone, let them go. If they're yours, they'll come back to you. If they don't, they weren't yours in the first place.' Some people find severing links painful and difficult, and resist at first. But when we can reach that place where we no longer love out of need, and release our hold on the objects of our attention so that they can come to us of their own free will, then we have learned to love unconditionally.

In Chapter 4 I showed you how to clear your personal relationship patterns with groups by sending out sound through the heart chakra. If at the end of your healing session you feel your patient has strong links with someone which need to be broken, or if there is still negative energy to be cleared between them, guide them through the following process.

Return to your patient's head and complete your healing session, then ask them to focus on your voice as they lie in a continued state of relaxation, eyes closed. Now name the person with whom they need to clear the energy. If they disagree or resist ask them to trust you, in the belief that whatever needs to happen will do so. If they can, they should make the sounds with you. Otherwise, ask them to join in silently, sounding the sound in their mind as you tone.

Now gently tune them in with a short sound meditation, bringing the energy up from *ah* at the root through the chakras to *ooh* at the crown. Next, bring the energy from the crown back into the heart with the sound *oh* and colour green. Ask your patient to imagine they are breathing sound and colour in and out through their heart centre with the continuing sound *oh*.

Now tell them to see the person concerned standing directly in front of them so that their heart chakra is in line with the patient's, and place an Angel of Sound behind this person. Quietly and purely begin to sound an *oh*, asking your patient to envisage a pure green light like a powerful laser travelling with the sound from their heart to that of the other person. They should see the linking sound and colour effortlessly beaming through the other person and out the other side to the angel, to clear and heal all pain and problems from the past.

To begin with, they may experience resistance as though the other person were blocking their passage. If so, speak to the higher self of the other person, asking for your patient to be allowed to clear the past in the spirit of love. Your patient may also discover, as they send this light and sound from their heart, that they have access to the other person's feelings and motivations. This will help them to understand that person's behaviour towards them. Tell them not to take any of the person's problems into themselves.

Continue with the sound *oh* until you intuitively feel all blocks are removed and the sound and colour are effortlessly flowing from one heart to the other. Then guide your patient to change the sound from *oh* to *ooh*, transforming the green to vibrant gold. Ask them to emit this new sound and colour strongly from their heart, seeing it go right through the person's heart and into the angel behind. Continue with the sound *ooh* and then tell them to see the angel returning this beautiful golden energy to them back through the other person's heart like a beam of solid gold light.

Now ask your patient to allow themselves to receive it fully, visualizing their heart chakra expanding more and more as they relax and bathe in the pure gold sound and light. Affirm that the wounds of the past are healed, and let them experience what it feels like to be acknowledged, loved and supported for who they truly are, with a sense of oneness with every created thing. Suggest that every cell of their body is experiencing this feeling of love as it effortlessly fills them, continuously beaming from the angel through the heart of the other person and into their heart.

Now change the sound to *ah* and ask your patient to look directly into the eyes of the other person. Ask them to observe if there are still any 'ties' growing from their body that link them to this person – for instance, from the eyes, mouth, hands, knees, breasts or sexual organs. Continue to sound the sound until your patient can clearly see all the ties. When they can, ask them to take an imaginary implement (anything from a pair of scissors to a chainsaw!) and cut these ties one by one. They may find some spring back immediately. Tell them to cut again. Others may be like tree trunks or iron girders. But they must keep on cutting until all are severed. Then ask the patient to remove their half of the ties from their own body and bury them in the ground.

Change back to the sound *oh*. Tell them to thank the other person for being in their lives and for what they have received from them – both the good and the bad. If they can, they should forgive them. Next, explain that it is time for them to be free of each other and to go their separate ways. As you tone, let your patient imagine the other person drifting away on the sound until they disappear completely. Continue to sound the *oh*, allowing your patient to experience in their body what it feels like to be completely free. Use the sound to empower them with this feeling so that they breathe it into their cells and vibrate with this new and vital freedom. Let it permeate their aura and fill the space around them. When this is completed, cease toning and ask them to open their eyes when they feel ready.

This is a very simple technique, but it works. Tell your patient to continue to use the sound with this visualization of cutting these ties over the next few weeks, to consolidate and enhance the work you have done together.

Empowering with Sound

Very rarely one is asked to do a sound session which turns out to be an empowerment of that individual. I say 'very rarely' because most people are still working through their patterns, and few are clear enough to receive 100 per cent that pure, energizing sound from what I have come to perceive as 'the highest ray of healing'.

Empowerment can only occur when someone is really clear in all bodies. Then the sound can be used to raise the vibration of that person higher and higher. This really is the 'sounding' of what we call the 'light body', where the grosser vibrations no longer exist and everything flows perfectly in harmonic unity. It is the creation of a being in tune with mind, body, spirit and emotions, and it is as joyful to give as it must be to receive.

You will know when it happens, because there are no lumps and stones and knots to remove – just a sending in of beautiful clear energy with the sound, and a toning of the chakras to resonate with the highest qualities of the higher self. These rare sessions are marked by their effortlessness and the purity of sound which flows from your mouth.

Releasing Emotional Patterns in Pairs

This is the process we went through in Chapter 4, only now you're going to do it with your patient. Once again, it is simple to do. Sit opposite your patient and hold both their hands. Have a box of tissues and a pillow nearby. Ask them to close their eyes and bring strongly into their mind the situation and person currently upsetting them, imagining it happening now so that their heart may start beating faster, their stomach may feel sick and their solar plexus full of butterflies.

When they are truly experiencing the situation on all levels, tell them to use any sound that comes to them. They may be reluctant at first, so help them by making sound with them, moving the pitch higher or lower until they find a sound that really resonates with them. Tell them to continue to hold the situation in mind and body and keep toning over and over, breathing as deeply as they can. Again, you can make the sound with them and even begin to rock back and forth with your bodies if you wish, still linking hands. Work with them, making the sound for as long as it takes, until they experience a sudden flash of connection and trigger back to the original situation which upset them in the first place.

Now work with them to help them express their feelings. Encourage them to yell, to scream, to cry, to pound the pillow, to hug it to them. If necessary take them in your arms and rock with them until everything has been released. When they have calmed down a little, use gentle, peaceful sound to heal that hurt place inside them. If they can join with you in toning, so much the better, and again it will be very helpful if you can write out an affirmation for them to chant or speak. People are often amazed to discover that someone who is 'pushing their buttons' now is mirroring a situation which happened many years ago and has still not been healed, and that once the situation is healed it no longer has power over them.

One final reminder: don't use this very powerful mode of releasing with partners in workshops, unless you have a great deal of support available for those who are clearing patterns.

The HPA Axis

I have left the HPA (Hypothalamus–Pituitary–Adrenal) Axis until last, because you won't become aware of it until you've been working with sound for some time. I had noticed that, when I was working on patients' feet and sending the energy up the body towards the crown, the nervous system stretched out before me in the legs, arms and torso like an intricate electrical map which lit up when sound energy hit it. As I sat at the feet, I began to use a process of 'clearing' the spinal column by pointing my hands in between the legs and aiming the sound at the root chakra in the base of the spine.

Beginning with a low tone and the sound *ah* I 'pushed' the energy up the spinal column to the next chakra, changing to the next tone up and the sound *ay*. I continued up the chakras, changing sounds and tones, until I reached the third eye. Sometimes, if the spine felt blocked, it took longer to move the energy up the chakras; on other occasions, with very clear people, the energy moved effortlessly.

When I reached the third eye chakra I began to raise the pitch of my tones, going higher and higher until I saw the energy move past the third eye towards the crown and begin to circle the two lobes of the brain in a clockwise motion. Higher and higher, stronger and stronger I made the sound, and faster and faster the energy circulated, until at a certain pitch the energy pulsed down like a bolt of lightning through the pituitary gland behind the third eye, down the nerve pathways to the adrenal glands, and from there out into the central nervous system, flooding energy through the entire body.

So clearly did I see this, time after time, that, with no medical knowledge of what I was doing, I drew a rough diagram and showed it to an endocrinologist friend. 'Ah yes!' he said. 'You're working with the HPA Axis.' If he'd said I was working with a boa constrictor I wouldn't have been any the wiser, so he gave me an article to read.

The HPA Axis is part of the brain's neuroendocrine response to stress. In layman's terms, there is an intricate mutual response network linking the immune system and the brain: electrical signals along nerve pathways are converted to chemical signals which affect behaviour and response to stress. The hypothalamus in the brain produces the hormone CRH (cortico-tropin releasing hormone), and releases it into a specialized bloodstream circuit that conveys it to the pituitary gland (just beneath the brain), causing the pituitary to release ACTH (adrenocorticotropin hormone) which in turn stimulates the adrenal glands to produce cortisol, the classic stress hormone that arouses the body to meet a challenging situation. But cortisol also modulates the overall stress response by inhibiting the release of any further CRH by the hypothalamus. Cortisol is also a powerful immunoregulator and anti-inflammatory agent. It acts on many parts of the immune system to prevent it from over-reacting and harming healthy cells and tissues.

Sending sound through the central nervous system:
My Rough Diagram

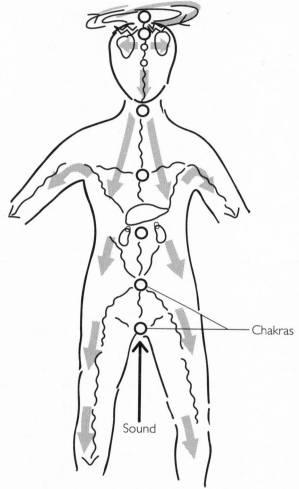

Sound circling the brain lobes as electrical frequency reacts at a
certain pitch with the hypothalamus and is converted to a chemical
signal which affects the adrenals and thence the immune system

My endocrinologist friend told me to approach it like yin and yang: homeostasis (an internal steady state of the body) relies upon perfect balance between the immune system and the HPA Axis. Disruption in any way (through drugs, surgery, toxic substances or inherited) exacerbates the diseases the two systems guard against: infectious, inflammatory, autoimmune and associated mood disorder. There is a growing body of evidence that impairment of the HPA Axis (and thus lower levels of CRH secretion) results in a hyperactive immune system, lethargy, fatigue and excessive sleep. It is interesting that patients with illnesses such as chronic fatigue syndrome, seasonal affective disorder and some types of depression also exhibit some CRH deficiency.

So exactly what was I doing with sound? My rough diagram showed that I was sending sound waves up the spinal column to stimulate the hypothalamus and create balance between the two lobes of the brain. At a certain pitch, the electrical charge of the sound stimulated the hypothalamus to send energy in a downwards motion to the pituitary gland, thence to the adrenal glands and from there into the central nervous system. I could not prove that I caused hormones to be released as I did this, but telepathically and visually this is what I saw happening. I was using sound to stimulate the production of cortisol, a hormone which in turn mediated the restraint of the immune response and induced behaviour that assisted in recovery from illness or injury.

What was even more fascinating was that the two patients on whom I had initially developed this technique were suffering from chronic fatigue syndrome, and I had intuitively felt that both their adrenal systems were in a state of exhaustion from continual stress due to an over-response to fear.

What I have described is a very powerful process which floods the body with highly charged positive energy. Be very careful to assess whether your patient is strong enough to receive it, and how high you can go with the tones. Begin gently, and build up in stages over a number of sessions. If you feel any resistance or adverse reaction as you move the sound higher up the spine, please stop. Don't forget how powerful you are, and how vulnerable people feel when they are chronically ill.

HPA (Hypothalamus – Pituitary – Adrenal) Axis

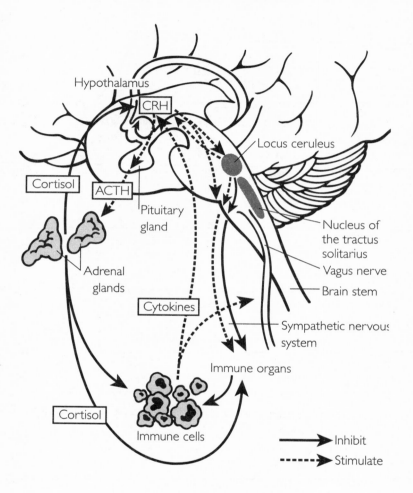

Hypothalamus

CRH

Locus ceruleus

Cortisol

ACTH

Pituitary gland

Nucleus of the tractus solitarius

Vagus nerve

Brain stem

Adrenal glands

Cytokines

Sympathetic nervous system

Immune organs

Cortisol

Immune cells

Inhibit

Stimulate

The Akashic Record

Honour the following information and use it wisely, for it is not lightly given to us by the angels. The Akashic Record, or Akasha, is the place where the records of every incarnation of every soul are held. According to Paul Solomon, a 'recording angel' allotted to each person keeps the records up to date with each new incarnation. On a number of occasions in very deep trance meditation I have perceived the Akasha as somewhere beyond 'the music of the spheres' and the angelic realms, located in a crystalline structure which seems to be suspended in space and time, and which looks similar to the structure of DNA molecules.

These records can only be accessed from the highest place of personal integrity and in compassionate service to the individual concerned. If not, the information which will come through is likely to be unreliable and influenced by the ego-personality of the enquirer, which will render it worthless.

Only ask for access to the Akasha when you have been working with sound for some time, when you have a strong link with the angels, and when you are clear, centred and able to put yourself aside fully in service to another human being. If you can honestly fulfil all these criteria, ask the Angels of Sound to take you to this place and admit you to the person's records in order to be given the sound that will completely heal that soul.

Access may be denied, but if you do gain entry many kinds of information can be received. On the three occasions on which I have been allowed in, I saw rather than heard the healing sound in the form of colour, light and structure. The actual physical sound is too pure to be audible to the human ear. What I perceived was that the sound, colour and vibration of each soul in the Akasha rotates in a clockwise circular movement, and that when the soul is incarnated into the human body this sound and colour form the iris of the eye, imprinting the soul's records in the eyes. This is why we often feel we are looking into someone's soul when we look deep into their eyes. If you have ever experienced a prolonged eye-to-eye meditation with someone, you will now understand why after a time you will begin to see different faces and incarnations flashing across their meditating face.

On one occasion I asked for the healing sounds from the Akashic Record for an entire group. The sound flowed into my body in a continuous stream of soft pink colour and, as I absorbed it, I felt all the pain and sadness which those souls had struggled with so deeply that the tears poured down my face. On another occasion I entered the record of a woman with chronic fatigue syndrome, and was surprised to observe that the energy within it was almost stationary. I used sound until it began to rotate in the clockwise motion once more, moving up the octave until I reached a pitch at which I felt the information energy in the record had stabilized. I then took that same pitch and worked with it on all the woman's energy centres from root to crown, creating a circular clockwise pattern over each one, ending with the eyes to reprogram the irises. It was very powerful and the left side of the woman's body responded strongly with tingling, pins and needles and some temporary discomfort as the energy moved.

It was also my perception that somewhere in the Akasha – very much like the Platonic theory of the universe whereby everything exists first in the form of the perfect idea – is the code for the perfect molecular structure of our DNA, and that, using sound, we can draw this into our bodies to rejuvenate and revitalize us back to health.

When you enter the Akasha, you will be required to work at the limits of your concentration as your focus must be laser-sharp. Paul Solomon found his frequent excursions extremely tiring as he came right out of his body and sometimes experienced difficulty in getting back afterwards. You don't need to leave your body to consult the Akasha, but you do need to leave your ego/personality behind. That is probably why very few continuously offer themselves from such a high place of commitment and service in order to channel, and I myself only ask for access on rare occasions and in exceptional circumstances.

Sound and Children

All the techniques described above are specifically for working with adult bodies. Remember that different chakras develop at different ages:

Chakra Development

Chakra	Age
root	birth to 3–5
sacral	3–8
solar plexus	8–12
heart	12–15
throat	15–21
third eye	21–26

Be aware of the power of sound on young children who are not yet fully developed and open. Gentle mid-pitched tones are the best for healing them, and what works really well is the sound bath technique, described in Chapter 6. You can also use sound-less sound, holding your hands over the affected area and silently toning the note inside you.

Children of all ages have participated in my workshops (see also pp. 106 and 114), and once you can get past their initial self-consciousness you will find they can intuitively understand and accept the power of sound. One little boy of six or seven was a joy to watch. He immediately 'felt' the power of the sound coming from his voice and hands, and his whole energy field lit up. He was a tiny master of sound, with such a natural ability to focus clearly that he led the older children with his stillness and intensity. I saw that he could work effortlessly with sound, and write these words now in the hope that the experience of the workshop will inspire him to continue, even though he is so young.

Passing Over Sounds

Pure gentle sounds can soothe and comfort the dying, and help them to pass over more easily. A colleague and I were called into a children's ward where a young boy with terminal cancer had been in a very weak state for some days. It was his birthday, and we bathed him in sound and love. His eyes spoke worlds, and shortly afterwards, he died.

You can also use silent or absent sound to support someone on their journey. My father was in hospital with a bad back and none of us imagined that he was going to die. I was abroad and suddenly felt his presence with me. In that moment, I had a premonition. I began to meditate and visualized the entire family sitting at his bed linking hands with him, and saw and heard us sounding beautiful tones to help him leave. I later discovered he had died at the very time I'd silently sent the sound. So do not be afraid to use your voice in this way to help others find peace.

Focus Work

It's always a good idea to keep case notes when you're working on someone over a period of time. This helps you to see not only how they have progressed, but also how you have developed. After each session, log all you can remember. This includes your feelings, apprehensions, anything you may have 'seen' with your inner vision and messages you may have received from the angels, as well as external physical reactions and comments from your patient. Keep a record of any releases that may have occurred, any ties you cut or affirmations you may have given. You will be surprised at just how much has been experienced with such simplicity and ease by using the sound of the human voice in tune with compassion and service, by both you and your patient. Miracles can happen. All you have to do is allow them in.

Chapter 6

THE CIRCLE OF SOUND: USING SOUND WITH GROUPS

By now I hope you will have experienced using sound on yourself and others. When you take the next step and begin working with groups, you will really understand the true meaning of 'surround sound' and its calming and healing properties.

You can use any of the exercises in previous chapters for breathing and warming up, and also work with the sound, colour and movements from Chapter 4. With larger numbers, people are less self-conscious about the sound of their own voice and therefore more likely to let go and sing out. There is also something magical about a large group making sound together, because sound instantly unifies, and the group vibration can become very powerful. It creates a support system and people often cry or even laugh spontaneously as the sound opens them up and inner feelings emerge.

I once worked with a group of teenagers in their music class with the chakra, colour and sound system. By the end of ten minutes' toning and breathing, they were very surprised (and one of them even slightly alarmed) at the energy tingling through them. It's a shame the current school system doesn't allow for teaching children how to make use of their own energy positively. Most of them have no idea they are able to take charge of their own 'powerhouse', and either allow it to explode at will or use toxic chemicals in the belief this is what they need to feel alive. If only they knew they could freely get all that and so much more, just by understanding and accessing their own power.

Here are a few ideas you can try with any group. As usual they are guidelines, so be inventive. Develop your own games, create your own chants, and most of all have fun!

The Ohm Circle

This is a great way for helping people relax and lose their inhibitions. Get everyone to stand in a circle, left shoulder facing in. Each person then places their hands on the shoulders of the person in front and lightly massages them, moving up and down the back at will, and ending by tapping gently up the backbone and neck to the crown, to help circulation. Then everybody circles their arms around the waist of the person in front, and the whole circle pulls in together in a closely knit hug until each solar plexus is pressed against the back of the person in front.

You may encounter some resistance at first, plus some nervous giggling, but be persistent. When the circle is really pulled in tight begin to sound an *ohm* together, if possible all breathing at the same time and choosing a low-pitched note, as the lower frequencies will vibrate strongly in the body. Ask everyone to imagine the *ohm* coming out of their solar plexus, going into the back of the person in front and continuing around the circle. When they have mastered this, ask them to imagine their backs opening up to receive the *ohm* from the person behind.

Continue with the *ohm* as long as you like. In fact, the longer you do it the more powerful it will become. Most people find this a very pleasurable and relaxing experience which generates a sense of support and oneness, helping people to bond with each other and the group.

Circle on the Floor

This time sit on the floor in a circle, left shoulder facing inwards, legs in a V-shape either side of the person in front. Ask everyone to place their two hands, palms flat, on the back of the heart chakra of the person in front (middle of the back, just below the shoulder blades). This time they're going to envisage sending the sound *oh* through their hands, right into the back of the next person and out through their heart, clearing and opening the entire heart chakra as the energy moves round the circle.

Once the process is under way ask them to add the colour green as they tone the sound. If you want to bring different qualities to the heart energy, you can gradually change the sound and colour. Continue sending both through the group as long as you like.

The first time I did this exercise with a group, I saw that the concentrated collective sound and heart energy was creating a pyramid-like structure in the empty centre of the circle. Immediately I sent a woman in the initial stages of multiple sclerosis to sit in the middle, and afterwards she said she had received wonderful energy from it. So if you have someone who particularly needs healing, place them in the centre and allow them to soak up the vibrations.

Sending Out Sunflowers

I also like to use sound in a circle with groups seated on chairs. The sound and colour chakra meditations from Chapter 4 work perfectly well in this more relaxed manner, and sometimes the support of a chair can help you to focus.

Once you have centred the group on their breathing slowly move up the chakras from root to crown, then direct the energy back into the heart with the sound *oh* and the colour green. (You can also use pink in the heart chakra, which is said to be the colour of compassionate love.) Use some of the techniques described in earlier chapters for sending out healing. Ask your group to hold someone in their mind's eye and use hands and sound together to transmit energy. They can also give healing to themselves by intuitively directing their own hands to where their bodies require it.

Next, let them visualize breathing in and out through their heart chakras to open them wide. Continue to sound an *oh*, seeing golden energy filling the space and creating a brilliant sunflower in the heart. Repeat the sound, changing it to another vowel if you wish, until the sunflower is rooted and strong. Then send it out to someone in need of love. Tell the group to imagine that person receiving it in their heart as they tone, and to see the joy shining on their faces.

Next ask everyone to link hands and use sound to create a sunflower within the whole circle, as though each person were an individual petal. Lift the imaginary sunflower with sound high above the circle to the ceiling. See it pouring light and golden energy on everyone. Then with the next sound move the sunflower into the sky above the town, like a huge flying saucer beaming light. With the next sound move it even higher into the sky, so that it shines radiance on the whole country. Finally, use sound to take the sunflower right out into space so the whole group is looking down on the planet. Imagine the rays of gold light from the sunflower reaching all those places which need love and healing. See endless effortless energy pouring down, creating harmony and peace wherever it touches the planet.

Continue making sound with your group for as long as you like, and gradually bring the sunflower back into the sky above you. See the energy pouring down into government buildings and on to the heads of politicians, and use the sound to fill their hearts with compassion and peace. Imagine what it would feel like to live in a country filled with that energy, working with that energy, inspired by that energy.

Finally, see the sunflower petals gently falling to the earth as you tone, going wherever they need to. As each petal touches the ground, a beautiful sunflower of love springs up. Use sound to envisage those sunflowers growing everywhere: in people's hearts and minds, in wild meadows and town gardens, in hospitals and schools and institutions. Finish by bringing a small sunflower back into each heart with the sound, and shrinking it until a pure gold ray of light shines from the heart centres of the whole group, linking them to each other and to the eternal source of love.

It may just be coincidence, but the first time I did this meditation in Slovenia, the group and I sent a sunflower of peace into the government buildings and to the head of state. Less than a week later, I was quite unexpectedly invited to meet the president's wife in those very government buildings we'd empowered. When you're using your heart in service, anything can happen.

A circular sunflower meditation with sound and prayers is also wonderful to harmonize a group before a concert. I've done this in the dressing-room with children's choirs, adult choirs, musicians and actors, raising the sunflower up above the theatre and sending the rays down into the hearts of the audience and finally bringing the sunflower back to radiate from the hearts of all the performers. It really helps to settle nerves by linking performer to performer, to audience and to the creative spirit.

Letting Go into the Pool of Light

This exercise was developed in my first support group. I also call it 'naming the name', because when we voice our fears in public we are acknowledging and confronting them. Facing our fears in this way takes courage and helps us to affirm that we are more powerful than they are. The exercise is probably best done with a small group, because going round a circle one by one takes some time.

Use the sound and chakra meditation to centre your group, and finish by bringing the energy back to the heart with the sound *oh*. Ask the group to close their eyes, join hands in the circle, and imagine they are breathing in and out through their heart centres as they tone. Each person then begins to send a gold beam of light from their heart into the centre of the circle, filling the space with gold energy and creating a beautiful healing pool.

Allow everyone to continue with the sound softly, lovingly and gently, and while the rest of the group focus the light in this way go round the circle one by one so that each person in turn stops singing and speaks out loud, stating, 'I let go of ... into the pool of healing light.' They should then discard whatever it is in their lives they would like to release – a situation, a feeling, an attitude, a place, a link to a person, a memory, an illness. After each person has 'discarded' into the pool they should affirm, 'So be it', as a cue for the next person to speak.

Continue round the circle until the group has nothing more to let go of. Change to the sound *ah*, move the pitch up slightly and ask everyone to see the negative energies in the pool transformed into gold light and drawn away by the Angels of Sound. Continue softly with the sound *ah* and go round the circle once more.

This time, ask people to call into their lives everything they want, need and deserve. You may need to reassure people that they really are allowed to ask for something for themselves, because, as you will discover in the next exercise, very few of us believe we are worthy of receiving anything at all, let alone what we really desire. Use the words 'I call into my life …' and again finish with 'So be it.'

Continue around the circle until the process is complete. Then tell the group to breathe the gold light into their bodies through every pore. Move the pitch higher again and change from *ah* to *I am*. Continue to chant *I am* for a few minutes, feeling this strong, positive energy in every cell, muscle, tissue, bone, nerve and fibre. Ask the group to unlink their hands and, before they open their eyes, to sit in silence and experience what it is like to be truly and freely themselves in heart, mind and body.

Giving and Receiving Sounds

I developed this simple exercise at a workshop where there was a lack of balance in the participants. Most of us find it far easier to give than to receive, because receptivity implies being open, and openness can be an extremely vulnerable state when you've experienced hurt or rejection. But many people who give too much don't understand how tiring it is to be with a person who doesn't allow others to give back.

We also need to release the widespread belief that it is selfish to do something for ourselves. In fact, the true meaning of being *self*-ish is not lack of consideration for other people, but learning to be responsible for our own needs. Until we can learn to love, support and give to ourselves, we cannot honestly give to anyone else. How often do we truly do something uncondition-ally? Usually there's an implied motive behind our simplest actions: we want someone to respect or like us, because when you don't respect yourself enough there is always a need for others to fill that empty hole inside you.

So it may be interesting to observe what effects the following exercise has on your group. People may suddenly see themselves in a different light when they realize they have difficulty in receiving. Then comes the next challenge: what are they going to do about the problem they've just discovered?

Split your group into two equal lines facing each other. Everyone should stand with arms bent at elbows, palms facing inwards, and practise sending energy from one hand to the other, using the sound *ah* and the colour red. Get the group to concentrate so that they can almost see the sound and colour streaming from palm to palm. Then ask everyone to turn their hands, palms facing out, towards the out-turned hands of the person opposite. Now, using the sound *ah*, each person should send the energy from their hands into their partner's. Again, ask the group to visualize and feel the sound and colour coming from their hands, crossing the space and going into the hands opposite.

Now we are going to use the chakra sounds as usual. The idea is to create a kind of tai chi flowing movement back and forth with the body as you send the energy out and release back. Try and feel a rhythm with the sound and movement.

Begin with Line A as the receiving line, Line B as the giving line. Line A should stand relaxed and motionless, eyes closed, breathing in through the nose down the 'channel of air' to the sacral chakra just below the navel. Line B sends the sound *ah*, stretching their hands towards the root and rocking forward on the outbreath. Inhale and rock back on the inbreath. Repeat three times, then reverse the roles, so that Line B receives and Line A sends the sound.

Continue this process up the chakras with the relevant sounds (*ay* to the sacral, *or* to the solar plexus, *oh* to the heart, *ee* to the throat, *ohm* to the third eye, *ooh* to the crown, *I am* to the whole body), reversing each time so that the balance switches between receiving and giving.

If you wish you can repeat the exercise again, adding colours to the sounds and chakras. See if you can invent your own ideas for sending and receiving sound within the two lines. Allow a few minutes after the exercise for people to discuss their experiences privately with their partners, and then in discussion with the group.

Sound Bath

This simple, effective technique works almost too well – people want to stay behind and be bathed over and over again! Many people fall asleep, while others cry, rock to and fro, or vibrate and shake. Because it's such a relaxing and therapeutic process, I usually leave it until the last section of the workshop.

I find it works best if everybody sits on the floor, but if some people need to stay in chairs make sure they direct the sound down towards where the recipients are lying. For optimum comfort over the five to ten minutes involved you will need some blankets or rugs in the centre of the floor for those on the receiving end to lie on, and a circle of cushions for everyone else to sit on.

I begin with one volunteer in the centre – someone who really feels they would like some healing – and gradually increase the numbers as people get the idea. The sound should be completely random. People can sing whatever notes they like, high or low, for as long as they like. The only thing they *must* do is all breathe at different places, so there is a continuous sound with no breaks in it. If the group wish to direct the sound towards the patient with their hands in any way, or send colour simultaneously, they may, but they must not touch the patient's body.

Before you begin, agree a cue for the toning to cease. I use a bell or drum. Also tell the group which vowel sound you have chosen to use, and ask them to stick with that particular sound for the duration. It's up to you to decide how long it lasts.

The sound may falter at first, but gradually it will build in intensity. If you have fifteen to twenty people randomly toning it really does sound like a choir of angels, with strange discords and beautiful harmonies appearing and disappearing at will. On one occasion we had a choir master participating in the work-shop. 'I spend hours rehearsing my choir to sing in tune together,' he said, with a mystified look on his face. 'The people in this group aren't even singers, and yet with no practice at all the sound is perfect!' The difference, of course, was that every-one who was toning had opened their heart energy in service and compassion for healing the 'patients' receiving the sound. We were in tune with our souls.

When your first 'patient' has come back to earth, it's useful for them to share what they experienced during their sound bath and to get feedback from those sending the sound. Now ask for some more volunteers to go in the circle – maybe two lying side by side, or three sitting upright, backs together, facing out to the circle. If you have time, continue until everyone has been both a sender and a receiver.

My most moving experience working with sound in this way was when a colleague and I were invited to work with a group of mentally disabled children and their parents. For the sound bath we placed six or seven parents in the centre of the circle, back to back, with their children sitting in their laps, so both parent and child were facing outwards. Everyone else made a big circle around them and began to tone.

I focused particularly on one little boy, seven or eight years old, but so weak that he could not raise his head, which was slumped on his chest. As I directed the sound at him gradually the little head began to move centimetre by centimetre, until some time later his head was erect, and he looked me straight in the eye. I empowered my sound with all the love I could find in my heart, and sent it to him, and I know that at some level he received it.

What we and the parents learned that day was that, though their children may not understand language, there is something about pure sound and vowel tones which communicates to disabled children: there was a response in their eyes. I have even found this at concerts, where the energy of my amplified voice very often seems to get disabled children dancing in their wheel-chairs. Words may not reach them, but heartsongs do.

Chanting, Drumming and Dancing the Sound

To chant together and move in rhythm while we work is quite alien to most people today, and exposing them to music and movement often sets up fear and resistance. In the seventies, working with the Kinks on their concept musicals, we were taught simple choreography by Dougie Squires (whose fashionable dance troupe The Young Generation was featured each week on TV's *Top of the Pops*). I was more than happy to stand on stage and sing, but getting the choreographed movements into my body was a huge problem and I spent rehearsals fighting back the tears.

Now I find a great sense of freedom in getting groups on their feet, stomping and chanting to the beat. Sometimes I'll use different kinds of taped music – many young people have never listened to classical music, let alone floated around a room following their basic instincts – and I alternate 'feels' and styles. I ask people to close their eyes, let the music flow through them, and echo with their body movements what the sound is saying to them. They can dance alone, in twos, in groups holding hands, or as an entire group in a circle.

Percussion instruments are great to get people going and remove inhibitions. Anything you can beat out a rhythm on will do – drums, tambourines, claves, triangles, wood blocks and, of course, your own feet on the floor. Begin by beating a strong four beat and getting the group to stamp from foot to foot, one two (right foot) one two (left foot) and so on, so that they really feel the rhythm in their bodies. Then start moving them round the room with the same beat, simultaneously incorporating percussion. Give them a while to get into it, then add a rhythmic chant.

There are so many chants you can use – just develop or discover your own. I really advocate writing your own words, finding a rhythm you like and using the chant to create or call whatever you want into your life, from world peace to health and happiness or a new partner. Or if you prefer, you can just use pure sounds to chant.

You can also chant someone's name for them. This is very empowering if you stand them in the centre of the circle and allow them to rotate as they receive the energy of their own special 'sound signature' – the vibration of their name.

Begin and end your group day with positive chanted affirmations and you will see how chanting clears the energy, not only of the people involved but also of the immediate environment. Combined with percussion and movement, it releases emotions and creates joy: letting go of the negative allows the life force energy to flow freely into that empty space. Eyes begin to sparkle, smiles form on lips and laughter bubbles up from within. It is impossible to be sad when you're chanting and drumming, because the beat pulls you back to the inherent rhythm of life and links you to the heartbeat of the earth.

CASE STUDY: My Father's Eyes

Healers often experience difficulty in working on family members, and I usually only do so when requested. In his late seventies, my father was diagnosed with a blood disorder called myloid dysplasia which meant his red blood cell count was gradually diminishing. His circulation was poor, his feet were swelling and his blood was slow to clot when he cut himself. An attack of pneumonia also affected his lungs and he found himself breathless, without energy and periodically attached to an oxygen cylinder.

My father had never been chronically ill in his life, and I have to say did not accept his illness with a good grace. However, he'd always had a powerful sense of mental visualization and decided he was not going to go down without a fight. In 1991 I was due to go to Australia on a six-week tour, and the doctor could not guarantee my father would still be alive when I returned. Knowing my father would suspect if I cancelled, I decided to go anyway; but we never told him how serious his condition was.

The power of visualization is well known, particularly in cancer patients, and he was determined to get better. His focus on self-healing became so intense that he literally 'was' his disease and could think or talk of nothing else. There were also times when he was overwhelmed with anger and negativity. His bedroom on occasions became particularly 'dark' and I often cleared the energy with my Indian drum and pure sound tones. Amazingly, he long outlived the doctor's prognosis, literally 'willing' his blood count back to normal and discarding the oxygen cylinder, the wheelchair and the walking stick. When he died five years later, it was from kidney failure which resulted in a heart attack, and his red blood count was normal.

Some months before he died, he complained of 'dryness' around his eyes and a fine, gritty powder which was a great irritant, causing him problems with his vision. His eyesight had in fact troubled him for years. I agreed to try some sound and was surprised at what I discovered. I knew that my paternal grandfather had been an Irish Catholic soldier in the First World War who survived the horror of four years in the trenches. He returned to London an atheist and, with no counselling available to alleviate the trauma, within a few years killed himself. It was Boxing Day, and my father was eleven years old when he returned from the cinema to discover his father dead, lying with his head in the gas oven.

I saw that the trauma of this situation had gone directly into the cellular structure of my father's eyes and remained there ever since. From that moment on, he was afraid to 'see' clearly. His heart centre was also traumatized and he had found refuge in his intellect, 'creating' in his life a highly successful unreal persona who functioned on reason and control and bore very little resemblance to the real man beneath. As I worked to release and transform the terrible childhood memory stored within my father's eyes, I was aware of his own father standing at his feet, asking forgiveness for all the pain his suicide had caused.

After the session I worked with my father to heal this relationship. When he finally opened his eyes, he was amazed to discover that he could see much better. His eyes were relaxed and less irritated, and his vision clearer and stronger. He also became aware of his tendency to go into his intellect, and made a conscious decision to try his best for the remainder of his life to stay in his heart when he dealt with people.

Sound Meditations

I always try to end my workshops with a twenty-minute sound meditation. It may seem a long time to tone, but it focuses and unifies the day and sends people out bright-eyed and energized.

Again, choose any vocal sound or word you like. It might be a sacred name like *Elohim* (an ancient Hebrew word for God) or *shanti* (meaning peace), or any of the chakra sounds. Alternatively you can use the basic chakra sounds for a twenty-minute chant, incorporating the quality of each chakra for focus. Just remember to enunciate the syllables clearly so that you experience the power of the vowel sounds. As leader of the group, you can also speed up and slow down the chant, as well as changing to higher or lower pitches. Decide whether you are going to take breaths in the same place and chant the sound in unison, or whether you are going to create a more 'angelic' sound by overlapping breathing and using random pitch of notes.

After your twenty-minute meditation close your group down as they will be wide open from the sound. The simplest and quickest way is that described on p. 74, of placing lotuses in each chakra and closing the petals tight, although I usually leave the heart slightly open.

There is nothing more fulfilling than observing people's faces after a day of sound together. You will never have seen such a peaceful glow and such sparkling eyes at the same time. The wonderful thing is that people leave carrying with them a new knowledge which they can easily make use of on anyone, at any time or any place. The truth is, we cannot sing this sacred sound without every single cell in our body joyously joining in. And when this pure vibration of love flows through the living temple of our body to fill our hearts, then we finally know and experience the true meaning of peace.

The Performer as Sound Healer

Any stage performer will tell you how it feels to gradually build up a rapport with the audience. To hold people's attention and emotions in such a way is a great responsibility, for there is an incredible power available to touch and inspire the individual. The performer has a unique opportunity to use his or her gifts for healing, because what is important is not the part you are playing, or even the words, but the sound of who you truly are behind that role. As I have said, the sound of your voice vibrates with everything you are in that moment – emotionally, mentally, physically, spiritually, etherically – and the more centred and at peace you are within yourself, the more energy you will have to lift and inspire people with your performance. So always prepare yourself by using pure sound or chanting before you go on stage. Attune to the highest in you, and this energy will vibrate in the timbre of your voice and leave a lasting impression on the audience. Know how powerful you can be in this: for if your performance that night reaches just one heart, if the sound of your voice touches just one life, in that single act you have achieved more than all the accolades and awards you ever dreamed of.

Chapter 7

CREATIVE WRITING WITH SOUND

One great gift my father gave me was frequently to tell me, 'Anything you want to do, you can.' So I was encouraged to sing, to play the piano and to write. From the age of five, along with my classmates I wrote and illustrated daily diaries and, with no television, became a prolific reader. I wrote poems, stories and essays effortlessly, and the words 'writer's block' were then unknown to me.

In 1981, when I became a professional writer for the theatre, a scary world of producers, directors and critics opened up, along with continuous rewrites, deadlines and eventually, my first opening night. But there was one thing that kept my mind fluid through all the creative ups and downs: meditation.

At first it was a great help, but then my periods of inner silence became a source of irritation. I would get everything prepared to begin writing and then sit quietly to do my meditation. As soon as I began to meditate, the ideas would start to flow. I would push them crossly to one side, saying to myself, 'I'm meditating. This is supposed to be my peaceful time, not work. Go away!' Then one day the penny dropped. The calm, rhythmic sound of my inner mantra was actually opening the doors of my intuitive creative energy. From that moment, whenever I was working on a project I went into meditation with a tape recorder, paper and pen beside me, because the ideas I was about to work on that day invariably expanded and developed as I meditated.

Later, I learned to understand it from a more technical point of view. We are all intrinsically creative, but most people are focused on left-brained logical processes. Not everybody makes maximum use of the right, intuitive side of the brain. The brain creates different electrical wave forms: beta in a normal waking state and alpha in a resting or drowsy state. Thus, most people produce alpha brain waves when they are inactive, in a state of relaxation (for example, when watching television). Creative people apparently produce a high level of alpha when they are working – that is, creating. Meditation is known to increase the regularity and amplitude of alpha waves. Thus mantras and meditation can align you even closer to your creative centre.

CASE STUDY: A Young Man in a Coma

Vincent was a brilliant young student who, tragically, had been the victim of a car accident on the day of his university graduation. For a month he had been in a deep coma and the doctors said he would never come out of it. The use of music to help coma patients is well documented, so I wasn't surprised to hear that Vincent's family had placed earphones on him, played him his favourite music, and read him stories plus the latest sports news for weeks on end. Then someone suggested they play him one of my CDs and, magically, a few days later he came out of the coma.

In no way am I suggesting it was because of me! Perhaps my pure sound was a catalyst, but I believe it was the love and support of his family that pulled him through. I was invited to visit Vincent and sing to him at the hospital. His head had been badly damaged. He could not speak and was partly paralysed, unable to get out of bed.

I decided to sing folk songs with my guitar as toning might appear unorthodox to the doctors, but when I reached any high notes I held them long and pure. Vincent's eyes were riveted to mine when I sang high, and I felt as though I was communicating directly with his soul. I also had the feeling that, although he couldn't speak to us, he could hear and understand. He was still in incredible shock in every part of his body, so I just used sound to soothe him.

I saw Vincent a number of times over the next two years, using sound to help release some of the accident trauma still in him. The most remarkable thing was his family, who mounted a twenty-four-hour support system of uncles, aunts and every available relation so that, even though he could not walk, he could eventually be at home. I think it is probably the most unconditionally loving thing I have ever seen.

Gradually through the remarkable work of a team of doctors and physiotherapists, Vincent did begin to walk. He still could not speak, but I knew he could think. He had studied electrical engineering, so I told him to imagine that the circuitry in his brain had been cut. Some of the nerve endings had been severed, and he had to use his willpower to see the 'electric cables' joining up and growing together again. He seemed to understand, and I told him to spend some time each day visualizing this. I also used sound to link nerves.

I have not seen Vincent for some time now. The last time we met he was able to sit at a table and feed himself, and use a computer to keep a diary. He had been working extensively with a speech therapist to learn to talk again. When I used sound on him, I was surprised to find his heart energy was now enormous.

Maybe I should not have been so surprised, because his heart was telling me that on one level he had chosen to have this accident. In the sacrifice he had made of himself, he had given his family the opportunity to learn what real unconditional love was – that we should not only love people when they are perfect and whole and easy to live with, but also when they are helpless, needy and difficult. I don't know many families who would have given so much, for so long, so tirelessly. And it is not over yet, for Vincent may never be able to look after himself.

I tell you this story for you to understand that sometimes when we work as healers, our patients have more wisdom, knowledge and teaching to offer us than we do them. So we become the pupil and they the master.

I believe we are born with our intuition wide open, but as we go through life we are gradually programmed to close it down. The poet Wordsworth states it perfectly in his 'Intimations of Immortality from Recollections of Early Childhood':

> Our birth is but a sleep and a forgetting
> The Soul that rises with us, our life's Star,
> Hath had elsewhere its setting
> And cometh from afar ...
> But trailing clouds of glory do we come
> From God, who is our home:
> Heaven lies about us in our infancy!
> Shades of the prison-house begin to close
> Upon the growing Boy ...
> At length the Man perceives it die away
> And fade into the light of common day.

The great Romantic poets of the nineteenth century used various drugs to try to re-enter this state of grace. But true creativity, which is an inner approach towards all areas of your life – work, play, relationships, health, living and even dying – doesn't need drugs or alcohol to express itself.

There is a misconception that creative artists produce their best work when stressed and impoverished. It's true that some people do flourish in stressful conditions. This, however, is their choice, not a necessity, and often the by-product of getting hooked on other kinds of drugs: adrenalin and struggle.

There is a better way, and sound can help you find it. Have you noticed how creators often fall in love with their creations? The novelist Charles Dickens hated completing a book, because he felt he had become so close to his characters that to be parted from them was like losing real friends. We need to be in this heightened state of unconditional love to truly create. We need to be open, receptive and linked to the creative unconsciousness. And I believe the simplest and most effective way of doing this is through sound.

I developed the following workshop when I was asked to participate in the annual Family Gathering of the Paul Solomon Fellowship, where teachers, mainly from America and England, led an interfaith international group for a week of workshops, lectures, concerts, therapies, exercises and excursions into the beautiful mountains which surrounded our hotel. You can work with the following techniques in isolation, or create your own workshop with a group. The group energy makes it a very powerful experience, but whether working individually or with others you will receive surprising insights into yourself and your own talents.

Inspiration from Nature

Wordsworth called himself a pantheist – like Native Americans, he saw and worshipped God in nature, and when I was designing this workshop I gathered natural objects from the countryside – leaves, flowers, coloured fruits, lichen-covered wood, fungi, pebbles, shells and seeds. I also added some interesting crystals of my own.

So to start with you need to forage in your local woods and fields. If you listen with your heart, things will speak to you. And remember, what may look like a simple boring twig to you may be a source of great inspiration to someone else. If you feel moved to pick something up, do so. When you have enough objects to give yourself a choice, or for everyone in the workshop to choose one, place each item in a separate paper bag and fold the top over so the contents aren't visible. Now you're ready to begin.

Let Go of Limitations, Fears, Judgments and Beliefs

Since creative thinking is really just a creative attitude towards every area of your life, we are all in a position to be wonderfully creative. So what stops us? Nothing but our preconceptions. It is the horror of the blank page. If we are an unwritten book, nobody can criticize us. As soon as we 'write' ourselves or scrawl the first few words on the manuscript we've become a visible target for attack.

So how do we change our attitude? We can do it by becoming

aware that we are co-creators with God (that is, the life force energy) in every moment. Each time we take a new breath we have a choice and an opportunity to begin again. Each time we take a new breath we are in tune with the abundant energy, the 'prana', that flows effortlessly through every living thing. How can we possibly feel empty when in reality we are always so full?

The process we are about to follow will help you discover what a world of creative imagination lies within you. Using sound, we are going to focus energy in the heart and then direct it on to the object from the paper bag you will randomly choose, so that you actually merge and become one with the energy of this object. Then you will write about it.

Before you begin, make sure everyone has paper and pen. Place your filled paper bags in a box or on a tray, and allow each person to choose one. If you're working on your own, take the one you are most drawn to. Open the bag and remove your object. Touch it, smell it, examine it. It may look solid, even dead or shrivelled, but it is vibrating with sound. You are going to tune into that sound and experience its vibrations, when you will discover that this object has a very special message just for you.

If you are leading a group, make it clear that the process of writing is not a competition or an exam. This is not a situation where 'more' means 'better', so don't be intimidated if in the time allotted you only write one word and the person next to you scribbles what looks like an entire novel. In this situation, even a blank page is meaningful and says something about the writer. Also make it clear that people can choose their own mode of expression – blank verse, poetry, prose, unrelated words and sentences, archaic language, modern slang, a foreign language, even a song lyric.

Work with the process described below, either on yourself or as a guided meditation to lead your participants in the workshop.

I Am Here and Now: Breathing

As you have already learned, your breathing is a simple way to anchor you back into the here and now. So sit quietly, holding the chosen object in your lap, hands relaxed, eyes closed. Once again, tune into the rhythm of your body organs and be aware of the breath as it enters through the nose, following it down the throat through the imaginary 'channel of air' between the lungs, all the way to just below the navel.

Breathe in gold light, and on the outbreath sound a low *ah*. Concentrate on releasing any fears you have about yourself. As you continue to tone, let go of any limiting beliefs, judgments, problems and worries. Visualize them carried away on the sound, and breathe self-confidence and vitality into the empty space left behind. Use the sound to clear those inner voices that say 'I can't' or 'It's not possible', and any blocks about your capabilities and projects. Continue this process until you feel totally released and regenerated.

I Am a Receiver and Transmitter of Ideas: Meditation

Now we're going to use the sound and chakra colour meditation to release any stress and tensions, to centre ourselves, and to balance the two sides of the brain. In that state of peaceful awareness we can enter the 'spaces' in between our thoughts where our true potential lies. Stay with each chakra and sound as long as you want until you feel ready to breathe the energy up.

Ah: Continue with the sound *ah*, focusing on the root chakra and flooding it with the colour red to energize and revitalize.

Ay: Now breathe the energy up to the sacral chakra with the colour orange and the sound *ay* for joyful new beginnings.

Or: When you are ready, on the inbreath pull the energy up to the solar plexus with the sound *or* and the colour yellow for self-confidence and trust.

Oh: Next is green as we breathe up to the heart chakra, emitting pure love with the sound *oh*.

Ee: This is the sound of truth and communication, as we breathe the energy to the throat with the colour blue.

Ohm: Breathe the energy up now to the third eye centre with the colour indigo and the sound *ohm* as we open to our intuition and inner seeing.

Ooh: From the third eye, breathe the energy up to the crown with the sound *ooh*. Visualize the crown slowly opening to let in the purple light of universal love. See yourself as an energy receiver into which positive thoughts and brilliant ideas can easily and effortlessly enter. Visualize the power lines of electrical thought which directly link the antennae of your brain to the highest channel of inspiration.

I Am Unconditional Love: Empathy

Now change the sound to *oh* and, as you do so, move your focus back to the heart chakra. See the sound emanating from your heart in a steady ray of pure green light. We are going to let go of the little self, the ego, and align ourselves with the creative life force that flows in and through everything. In this way we can become co-creators with God.

Still with your eyes closed, in your mind's eye picture your object and send the sound from your heart directly to it. Bathe it in sound and colour. Now, continuing to tone, slowly open your eyes and look at the object. Next, add the intention of unconditional love to the sound you are sending. From your open heart, channel a love so pure that you actually become that object. Feel its vibration, its rhythm, its life force and its absolute essence until you lose all sense of self and become the object. Keep sending the sound until you feel this total unity, then allow the object to 'speak' to you.

This object holds a wisdom for you alone, a gift to give, a truth to share. Open yourself to receiving what the object has to tell you, and when you are ready stop toning and begin to write it down. Find your own language and words. Allow the words to pour into the empty receptive vessel that is you and find expression in your loving consciousness.

At this point give your group a deadline such as 'You now have five/ten/fifteen minutes in which to write'. The process may open people to parts of themselves they have long closed off, so be prepared for tears. Only assist in an emergency, as it is important for people to experience their emotions and write about them. Occasionally you may notice someone not writing at all. Support them, asking them to get in touch with what they are feeling and what it is in them that doesn't want to be expressed. That in itself can be something to write about. If they are looking at a pebble and saying, 'This is stupid. It's dead and meaningless', they are clearly making a statement about a part of themselves. Encourage them to look deeper and explore.

If your workshop is disturbed by noise, tell your writers to use the feeling of annoyance or elation or whatever the noise brings up in them. Sometimes I'll walk round the room softly beating my Indian drum while people are writing, to relax them further, or gently pick the guitar. If you want to create an ambience to write with, make sure it is unobtrusive and not distracting. Naturally created sound is better than pre-recorded music.

Give a clear signal to end the writing, and then ask your participants one by one to stand in front of the group, holding the object they have written about for all to see. Allow them to share what they felt and experienced, and then ask them to read what they have written. They may take some persuading, as many people are shy of speaking in public and some of their insights may have been personal. However, if you can get the participants to do this it is well worth the effort. Everyone will be touched by the beauty and truth of what has been written, and many people will have had joyful experiences with positive realizations about themselves.

Sometimes people have deep insights which cause them to cry so much that they find it impossible to write. If this happens, encourage them to stand up and try to share their feelings.

At one workshop, a woman drew four tiny fir cones from her bag. Three were attached to a small twig, while the fourth had broken off. When she tuned in with her heart energy and the sound, she saw the cones were a message from her dead child. Like the cones on the twig, three people remained attached to life on the planet – the two parents and the other child – while the fourth had become separated from them. Yet although this child was dead, and the cone broken off, it still remained with the other three cones. The single separated cone showed the woman that the spirit of her dead child was still with them and that the bond of love would never be broken. She could not write this down, but she shared the story with us and left that day with a wonderful insight and gift.

If you are working on your own, give yourself a deadline. When you have finished, read what you have written and discover what you have learned about yourself. If you want to develop your ideas further in the next section, choose another bag and repeat the process with a new object until you have completed two or three pieces of writing.

People are continually amazed at the depth and quality of the writing they produce when they use sound. And if you can get so much from an inanimate object when you tune into it with your heart and unconditionally love it, think how much you could get from a human being if you did the same thing! How different would our relationships be if, every time there was a problem or a block, we went into our own hearts, focused on that beam of light and loved the other person more than we loved ourselves? If we used our power to link so completely with them that we understood and empathized exactly with what they were going through? Try it.

Ideas are building blocks

When everyone in the workshop has spoken or read, choose three or four pieces and try to fit them together into a story-line. Get the writers to stand in a line and read their pieces consecutively. It doesn't have to involve characters or even situations: you are painting pictures with ideas, linking them to create a landscape.

Reverse the order of the readings and see what difference this makes. Then completely swop the order around and see how this creates a different story again. Involve everyone in the workshop as much as possible, encouraging them to participate by adding their own readings if they wish, or replacing the initial ones. Continue for as long as you like.

If you are working on your own, select two or three pieces you have written in their entirety and place them in an order which is meaningful to you. Reverse and change the order to create alternative stories and word pictures. If you have only written one piece, focus on exactly what that is saying to you and about you and find a way to work with it and incorporate it into your life.

I Am a Clairvoyant: a Clear Seer

Although clairvoyants are regarded as highly gifted presagers of the future, we all have this 'clear seeing' ability within us. We just don't use it. But when we go into a state of meditation using sound and colour we can leave behind our everyday perceptions and senses, and 'see' through the eyes of our higher self.

In the preceding exercise we experienced the one-ness of everything through total unity with a natural object. We learned that by projecting love on to something, we can merge with it and understand its essence. This time we are going to use the sound and colour chakra meditation to tune into ourselves and see our own visions by looking through our third eye. Again, if you are leading a group make sure everyone is prepared with pen and paper. Use the following as a guided meditation, and stay with each chakra and sound as long as you want until you feel ready to move the energy up.

Ah: Close your eyes and focus on the root chakra with the sound *ah* and colour red to energize and revitalize.

Ay: Now breathe the energy up to the sacral chakra with the colour orange and the sound *ay* for joyful new beginnings.

Or: When you are ready, on the inbreath pull the energy up to the solar plexus with the sound *or* and the colour yellow for self-confidence and trust.

Oh: Next is green as we breathe up to the heart chakra, emitting pure love with the sound *oh*.

Ee: This is the sound of truth and communication, as we breathe the energy to the throat with the colour blue.

Ohm: Breathe the energy up now to the third eye centre with the colour indigo and the sound *ohm* as we open to our intuition and inner seeing.

Ooh: From the third eye, breathe the energy up to the crown with the sound *ooh*. Visualize the crown slowly opening to let in the purple light of universal love.

Continue with the sound *ooh* and focus your energy back down to the third eye in the centre of the brow. Keeping your eyes closed, envisage the third eye opening wider and wider so that you can clearly see with it. Imagine you are standing in front of a huge crystal pyramid. See the shape, size and colour as brilliant light hits it and is reflected back on to you. A door in the pyramid opens and you enter.

The pyramid is filled with rainbow-coloured crystals of all shapes and sizes. The effect is inspiring. You stand in the centre of the pyramid, drawing into you the multicoloured crystal energy. The roof slowly opens and a shaft of brilliant light pours down as you feel your crown opening to receive the energy. As you continue to tone, see this light flowing down into your third eye centre and shining out from it into the pyramid like a torch beam. The light is so powerful that you project it on to the facing wall and a large circular window appears. As you focus on the window, it magically opens to reveal a picture.

This picture can be anything: a person, an object, a landscape, a colour. Continue to tone as you allow yourself to see clearly through your third eye, taking in every detail of your creation. Let your imagination lead you on a journey of discovery and create whatever you want.

When you can picture the whole scene in detail, stop toning, open your eyes and begin to write, describing everything you saw. Again, give yourself or your group a deadline, and if you wish, create a peaceful musical ambience in the background for them to write to.

When everyone has finished writing, as before ask people to discuss their experiences with the group, reading out all the pieces one by one, and choose three or four to link together into a word collage or storyline. Remember to play around with the reading order to create different storylines. The writing will have a different energy from the first exercise, but will be interesting and revealing in its own way.

I Am a Master Builder: Storyboard Your Creation

'Storyboarding' is a technique by which, through a sequence of pictures, words or both, you can develop a situation and a set of characters into a fully fledged story. If you're leading a group, get everyone to write a 'character' on a piece of paper (teacher, politician, musician, tramp, clown and so on). Place all the characters in a hat and let everyone randomly draw one. If you draw your own suggestion, replace it and try again. Split the workshop into small groups and give each half an hour or more to create a story, using the characters they have drawn and including an excerpt from both of the pieces each person has written. At the end of the allotted time, each group will perform their piece.

If you're working on your own, decide on two or three characters you find interesting and, using the pieces you wrote from your sound meditations, create your own story around them.

The story may be written in any form – as a play with characters, a poem, blank verse, prose or song. Explain to everyone the process of mapping it out with a storyboard, using the following very basic headings:

Beginning	To set the scene
Middle	As a point you are working towards
End	As the conclusion
Characters	Who take part in and create the action
Storyline and setting	What happens during the whole piece and where the action takes place
Plot	How it happens and to whom, including any conflicts and resolution of problems

Go round each group as they work to see if they need help or encouragement. End with the performances, and ask for positive feedback from the 'audience' groups on how the piece could be expanded or improved. If you are working on your own, when you have written your piece read or perform it to someone you can trust – acknowledging your work in this way is an important part of honouring your own creativity to yourself.

Finally, ask everyone to work with their own individual writings over the next few weeks, either before going to bed or on getting up, to discover what their higher self is communicating to them and how they can incorporate this into their daily lives.

Chapter 8

MEDICINE SOUND ANIMALS

As the Native American aspect of this chapter appears rather out of the blue it may be helpful if I explain how and why I was led in this particular direction. The idea of aligning Native American medicine animals and their properties with sound is something that came to me gradually, rather like my Indian path itself.

My Acupuncture Indians

When I was a child in Wales, I headed for the hills, running barefoot across the fields whenever I could, and my favourite place was sitting beneath an oak tree, gazing at the mountains like an Indian. But real Indians were something you saw on the television. Apart from the Lone Ranger's side-kick Tonto they seemed to behave pretty badly, always accusing the white man of 'speaking with forked tongue', constantly getting drunk, and liable to scalp you the minute you turned your back. So I was totally unprepared for the events of early 1991. The previous year I'd been on tour in England in the stage version of the cult Australian melodrama *Prisoner Cell Block H*. Our director, Stewart Trotter, was newly qualified as a traditional Chinese acupuncturist and insisted he could make a new woman of me.

The first four sessions were quite amazing as my body began clearing energy, but on the fifth session I went into a trance as soon as he put the needles in. I astral-projected out of my body, and became a star in a twinkling firmament of heavenly bodies.

I was quite aware I was a star, and for a moment felt afraid at existing in eternity in such a form of just being. Then I realized I was part of the astral body of the universe, shining and beating to my own rhythm, suspended in timelessness, and I felt immense peace.

In a flash the scene changed. I was back on earth, decked out in buckskin, beads and finery, lying on a kind of bier. I knew I was young, but I had no idea if I was dead or alive. Indian braves wearing white feather headdresses surrounded me. Their chief was immensely wise and centred. 'Fly like the eagle,' he told me. 'Be as soft as a doe, as strong as a beaver, as clear as crystal springwater, as blue as the sky, and as fresh and green and luscious as the new shoots of grass as they grow.' I truly experienced what it felt like to have an entire tribe who respected, appreciated and approved of you. The Indians gave me a white feather which floated down and became a curly white streak of hair on my right brow. When I came out of my trance at the end of the acupuncture, I almost expected to see the streak in the mirror.

Over the next few months my 'acupuncture Indians', as I called them, appeared every time Stewart stuck the needles in. He said later that he was often aware of presences with me, but didn't know what they were. Amazingly, I could clearly remember everything the Indians said, and secretly wrote it down when I got home. There were some wonderful insights. 'To be an Indian princess,' the chief told me, 'to have a prince, you must be a princess from within. Pay no attention to exteriors. Be a princess from the inside out!' Another time he told me, 'To win the heart of a man, you must be like a spring flower.' As he spoke I clearly saw a yellow flower, like a celandine. It was golden, bright and open, but the main thing about it was its stillness. 'Be still and centred, loving and pure,' continued the chief, 'so that he may clearly see you and be drawn to you by your stillness and your perfume. Then he will pluck you for himself.'

I mentally asked about my singing because work seemed to have dried up. 'Sing the song of the wind and the waterfall,' said the chief. 'Sing like a bird.' At that exact moment a bird in the garden began to pipe clear and true. 'Sing for the pure joy of being alive.' I saw how my professional focus had become singing for money, instead of for the love of music and the expression of the self. I realized there could still be music in my life, whether I was paid or not. So I made a decision to go and sing wherever I was asked to, and to express the music in me in service to the planet and to other people.

On other occasions I was surrounded by Indian women, long dark hair framing smiling faces, as they softly sang. Once I was a child, rocked from side to side in a kind of cradle. They showed me a young girl of about eight, beautifully dressed, calm and peaceful. 'Can you not see how beautiful the child is?' they asked. 'Can you not see how deserving she is of being nurtured, looked after and cared for?' Yes, I could see. My eyes filled with tears. The child was me, and I was still trying to learn how to love and support myself.

The chief had more insights for me. He showed me the bright moon behind a cloud at night. 'See,' he said. 'The moon is ever beautiful, but obscured by a cloud. Then the cloud passes and for those who could not see before, they perceive the beauty of the moon. It was there all the time – only they could not see it. You are the moon.'

Another time the women brought me an Indian doll, like a corn dolly, and placed it on my stomach. Somehow it crossed the skin and was taken inside to become part of my abdomen. Then, with sagebrush, they began to cleanse me from head to foot. This was definitely women's work. I knew intuitively they were wiping away all vestiges of any man within me, smoking out and cleansing each area with the fragrant burning brushes, to prepare me for my husband. They delighted in the work they were doing.

The women sprinkled me with water, as with a blessing: drops on my eyes 'to clearly see him', on my lips 'to speak of love', on my heart 'to love him truly', on my abdomen 'to bear his children', on my feet 'to walk you towards him', on my lips and tongue 'to kiss and caress him', on my hands 'to hold him', on my arms 'to encircle him', on my nose 'to sweetly smell him', on my ears 'to hear him', and finally all over my aura to make it shine and sparkle 'so that he will see you and be drawn to you'.

It was a real 'preparation' ritual and dedication ceremony. Finally, the women scattered seeds like oats over me, and I lay covered in the gleaming brown kernels.

Sometimes it was a cold white landscape I saw, hills of snow and stark, leafless trees. The Indian chief said, 'Even in the times when the outlook is bleak, conserve your energy, for spring will surely come again. Tap into the life force as the tree does, with roots going deep into the ground.' He told me to hug trees when I needed energy, particularly the masculine kind I was missing at that moment, and to draw my energy from the source of the earth through the tree. 'And, will you fight to save the earth?' asked the Indian. My eyes filled with tears. 'Yes,' I replied. 'But how am I to do it?' 'You will be shown how,' said the chief. 'Sing the song of the sacred white buffalo, and help will come.'

At that time I knew nothing about the legend of the White Buffalo Calf Woman who brought the pipe of peace to the Indian nation, but some months later I came across a book in a shop and bought it out of curiosity. I wrote the 'Song of the Sacred White Buffalo' almost immediately, and help did come, in many ways.

Randomly switching on the radio one day, I tuned into a woman's voice saying, 'And in my dream, the Indian told me to fly like an eagle.' I froze on the spot. It was an interview with some women who had organized an exhibition in central London. All of them had had similar spiritual experiences of Indians which had inspired them to write, weave, bead, create and work with the native crafts. Within half an hour I was there talking to them. 'I thought I'd gone mad,' I confessed. 'I didn't dare tell anyone about the visions I had in my acupuncture sessions.' The women explained that, before the Indians were virtually wiped out, they had said that when the earth needed them they would come back to help. Wherever there was an open heart, an open mind – an open channel – they were sending the knowledge through. It was as simple as that.

It made sense to me. Why else would a rock singer from Wales end up on stage chanting in Sioux, praying for peace with the white buffalo and reminding audiences to thank the Earth Mother daily for everything she gives them?

Since then, my Indian path has continued as my commitment to serving the planet has grown. I experienced two past lives, one as the Indian wife of Running Moon, the peacemaker in my tribe, another as a ten-year-old child who stood and sang to Great Spirit while the 'blue-coats' massacred the tribe around me. I was called Singing Heart. Whether or not these were past incarnations I will never know. All I do know is that I experienced the intensity of those souls as though they were mine, and now it feels perfectly natural to find myself combining my two favourite preoccupations into one discipline. I call it my medicine sound animals.

As usual I began by working on myself, but my ideas swiftly accelerated when I was invited to lead a workshop for children and their foster-parents. When I discovered that the youngest there would be only seven years old, I was concerned that some of my sound techniques would be too sophisticated. But I knew that, even if I couldn't communicate with them, the sound animals would speak in some way. And I was right. The only thing I didn't expect was just how much the teenagers and adults would love the sound animals too.

Finally, I developed them into a system allied to my sound and chakra meditations. You may find some animals in unlikely places. Although Eagle signifies spirit and is aligned to the mental plane of Air, I have placed Eagle in the throat. In doing so, I have 'grounded' Eagle's higher mind by bringing it into the body to help us express our own individual truth with the Eagle cry of *ee*. I believe that, if you work with these animals, they will each bring you a gift in the relevant chakra. However, if you feel any resistance to my system be creative and design your own.

You can use these sound animals on yourself, you can share them with a group, or you can teach them to your children. Both fun and powerful, they are everlasting friends. On p. 158 you will find a very simple song with different lyrics for each animal. I've written these specially because singing is such a delightful and easy way to remember the individual properties of the animals, and you can also use them as sung affirmations when you're working with that particular animal's medicine.

Some of the postures are based on very simple yoga, so warm

up with a few stretches and wear loose clothing. You're trying to let go, and you don't want to be restricted in any way. If you're not used to holding postures, give your arms and legs a rest in between animals. Also, as most of the postures require you to sit with legs tucked under and knees bent in a V-formation, if you have any problems with your knees or find the positions uncomfortable sit on a strong upright chair (with the exception of Snake where you lie on the floor) and perform the exercises with the upper half of your body only. They will still be extremely effective.

The medicine sound animals can be used individually or in sequence one after another as a complete sound and chakra postural meditation. We are also working to release our problems into the abundance of Mother Earth. Don't forget she will always be pleased to receive your prayers of thanks in acknowledgment for her help.

One final thing. We should never take for granted what a joy and gift it is to be alive, and what an extra-special gift it is to have an animal friend beside us to help us on our journey. So have fun!

Frog: Cleansing

Sound: ah
Chakra: root
Colour: red
Energy: life force

Lyrics:

I sing to call the rainfall
Wash away the mud and slime
Clean and fresh, I swim through life
Alive and in my prime
Sing froggy, sing *aah*
Sing froggy sing, *aah*

Properties

Frog can swim in the pure clear water of life, or get bogged down in the mud. Water symbolizes our emotions, and Frog's song brings sweet rain to purify us, washing away our negativity and replacing it with vibrant clear energy. With Frog we learn to honour our tears, knowing that in shedding them we let go of the past and purify our soul in the present. Use Frog medicine to refresh and cleanse yourself by releasing anything that does not bring you peace or no longer feels appropriate to carry with you. Frog is a wonderful energizing way to start the day and swim freely through your life.

Position

Kneel on the floor, legs tucked under, feet beneath your seat and knees as far apart as is comfortable to create a V-shape. Form a triangle shape with your hands, so that each forefinger forms one side and the two thumbs touch tips to form the base. Then place your hands approximately 20 cm (8 ins) in front of you side by side on the floor, palms facing down. Very slowly lean forward and let your torso bend between your open knees until your elbows touch the floor. Now place your hands in the triangle shape flat on the floor. Slowly lower your head on to the triangle, resting your brow centrally upon it, so that your face is flat on the floor and your thumbs lie gently either side of the bridge of your nose. Breathe in the colour red deeply to the root chakra, and slowly exhale, each time allowing your body to relax into the position a little more. If you find this position uncomfortable try bringing your knees in closer together.

Silently call upon the energy of Frog to be with you and feel the rain begin to wash over you. Breathe in again, and on the outbreath begin to sound an *ah*, focusing on the root chakra. Continue to breathe in cleansing breaths and breath out *ah*, imagining that everything you want to release is pouring with the sound from your root and straight into the earth. See it all draining away. Pause for a while in your toning, and experience the silence. Be aware of how your body, your mind and your emotions feel. If you feel any tears or anger rising, let them out. Feel the purity of water washing away all rubbish from your life. Start the *ah* again and alternate with periods of silence until you feel completely cleansed and at peace.

Frog Position

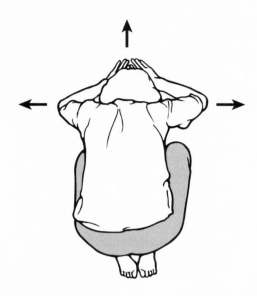

Snake: Life Changes

Sound: ay
Chakra: sacral
Colour: orange
Energy: joyful new beginnings

Lyrics:
> I shed my skin, transform myself
> I leave the old behind
> The way to change the outside
> Is to simply change my mind
> Sing snake, please sing *ay*
> Sing snake, please sing *ay*

Properties

Our patterns can become an invisible skin surrounding us, and Snake can help us to shed the old ways and transmute in the endless cycle of life, death and rebirth of our inner selves. The challenges of life can be dangerous, but by living through the poisonous 'snake bites', we can discover a fresh lease of life and become a new person. If we continue the process of release, peeling off the skins of the old 'us', wholeness will finally be achieved. Use Snake to let go of outmoded behaviour and reveal the real you underneath. Snake is extremely useful when you are trying to meet your challenges by changing old habits, and when you want to clear the past and affirm who you now are.

Position

Lie flat on the floor, stomach facing downwards, legs extended side by side to the back with toes pointed, and arms extended forward forming an arrowhead with palms together. Rest your head in between your arms so that the forehead and face are supported by your inner elbows and your nose and chin just brush the floor. Stretch your body from top to toe, then breathe in deeply and exhale, allowing your body to relax a little more with each outbreath. Experience the full length and streamlined shape of yourself as you lie in this position.

Silently call upon the energy of Snake and feel your skin begin to peel off you. Now breathe in the colour orange to the sacral chakra, sounding an *ay* on the outbreath and allowing it to resonate through your lower abdomen. Continue to breathe in deeply and breathe out *ay*, imagining that layers of old patterns are being shed from your body as you become lighter, clearer and more streamlined with the sound.

Pause in your toning, and experience the silence. Be aware of how your body, mind and emotions feel. Hold any situations that are difficult for you in your mind's eye, sound the *ay*, and see the old patterns fall from you like old skin, gently disappearing in the earth. Continue wth the *ay* again and alternate with periods of silence until you feel you have transmuted all the 'poison' in your life into positive energy inside you. Use the sound to remove the old and allow the emergence of the new. Something beautiful is about to be born!

Snake Position

Rabbit: Facing Fears

Sound: or
Chakra: solar plexus
Colour: yellow
Energy: clarity, courage, open to new possibilities

Lyrics: I call my fears out loud
And then I face them one by one
Living in the present tense
Means life is filled with fun
Sing rabbit sing *or*
Sing rabbit sing *or*

Properties

Rabbit is constantly on the look-out for danger, ready to high-tail it at the slightest threat and disappear into the dark safety of the burrow. The problem with being continually on the alert for disaster is that we emit fear and worry from every cell in our body, and even if we run away the pain and difficulties don't magically disappear. In fact, our fear of what *might* happen (and often never does) is the greatest negative meditation on the planet. Sacred law says that whatever we truly fear will surely appear in our lives as a lesson to teach us, because only when we confront our fears face to face can we become master of ourselves. Rabbit, constantly at the mercy of nature's predators, lives in a state of perpetual fear which attracts life and death challenges to be dealt with immediately. Rabbit offers you a choice: find your courage or flee. Use Rabbit as your greatest friend when you have a difficult situation to face or feel threatened by someone's attitude to you. Call your fears to you and face them by naming them out loud.

Position

Kneel on the floor, legs bent under, knees as far apart as is comfortable to create a V-shape. Lean slowly forward and place your hands with fingers splayed approximately 20 cm (8 ins) in front of your knees, shoulder-width apart with palms flat on the floor. Keep your arms straight and your head raised so that your eyes look directly ahead. Now close your eyes. Breathe in deeply, pulling the energy up to the solar plexus with the colour yellow, and as you breathe out allow your body each time to relax into the position.

Rabbit Position

    Silently call upon the energy of Rabbit to be with you, and as you do so name your fears out loud. Breathe in again, and on the outbreath begin to sound an *or*, focusing on the solar plexus. Now visualize right in front of you the person you are so afraid of, or what is causing you so much worry. As you breathe in the cleansing breath clearly see the person or situation, then breathe out with the sound *or*, using it to clear all fears and worries from this centre. Continue until you feel you have released everything from your body and allowed it to pour into the earth. Pause for a moment in your toning, and experience the silence. Be aware of how your body, mind and emotions feel. If you want to express anger, beat the earth with your fists like Rabbit thumping out a call. If you want to cry or yell, scream out your feelings like Rabbit's high-pitched squeal of anguish. Remember, if you try to control your fears, you may become them. Let it all out!

    Once you have released everything continue to tone, this time visualizing the sound emanating from your solar plexus as an empowerment of your true energy. Feel your strength and power as it pours from you to transform the other person or situation. Continue as long as you like, until you see the yellow turn to pure solid gold and you know that you are indeed an alchemist, with the power to change your greatest fears into your greatest achievements.

Deer: Loving Kindness

Sound: oh
Chakra: heart
Colour: green
Energy: harmony, love

Lyrics:

Gentleness of heart is mine
I live in harmony
I love the shadow and the light
In you as much as me
Sing gentle deer *oh*
Sing gentle deer *oh*

Properties

Deer, unlike Rabbit, knows no fear, using the qualities of love and compassion to heal and harmonize any situation. Deer's coat, with its light dapples stippling the dark, shows us that true balance means accepting both the shadow side and the light in ourselves and others. The best way to change a situation or a person is by changing our attitude towards them. Instead of using insistence and force, follow the path of sensitivity with Deer. Gentleness of heart, thought, word and deed will help us to heal not only our wounds, but the pain of others. By opening our hearts to the vibration of pure love, we can create peace and harmony in all areas of our lives. Deer's medicine of loving compassion will help you heal the sadness in any situation when your heart or someone else's feels tender or unloved.

Deer Position

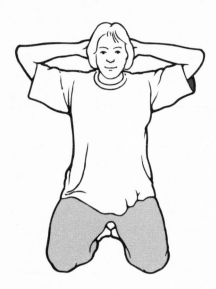

Position

Kneel on the floor, legs bent beneath you, knees slightly apart. Sit so your weight is centred over your heels, with your back relaxed and straight. Place your hands at the back of your head above ear level, palms spread and middle three fingertips touching, so that your elbows stick out either side to represent ears.

Now experience the stillness of Deer, unafraid and in harmony with every living thing. This position will really help you to open in trust. Breathe in the colour green, pulling the energy up to your heart chakra, and slowly exhale, each time allowing your body to relax into the position a little more. Breathe in again, silently calling upon the energy of Deer to be with you, and on the outbreath begin to sound an *oh*, visualizing the sound and colour pouring freely from your heart. Continue to inhale cleansing breaths and exhale *oh*, allowing your heart to be purified of all sadness, pain and anger as it releases from you into the earth. Feel the energy of deep compassion as it heals your wounds, allowing you to accept every weakness and fault as an integral part of yourself. Pause for a while in your toning, and experience the silence. Be aware of how your body, your mind and your emotions feel. If you want to cry, or laugh with joy, do so.

Start the *oh* again and alternate with periods of silence until you feel completely cleansed and serene. If you have a situation that needs healing send the colour and sound directly to it, creating a circle of light and love to transform it. If it is a person, visualize the sound travelling from your heart to theirs. As you enter their heart energy, you may experience their fears and problems too. Do not take these into you, but accept whatever you find with compassionate understanding. Hold to your quality of inner stillness and continue to tone until you are gently giving and receiving in perfect harmony.

Eagle: Spirit

Sound: *ee*
Chakra: throat
Colour: blue
Energy: truth of higher self

Lyrics: On wings of truth I soar so high
                 I'm powerful and strong
               With courage and clear spirit
               I find freedom in my song
                  Sing eagle, sing *ee*
                  Sing eagle, sing *ee*

Properties

Flying with ease between the limitless skies and holy Mother Earth, Eagle knows what true freedom is. A pure, free spirit, yet

Eagle Position

strongly connected to the earth, Eagle has passed many tests of initiation and now sees with piercing eyes a new vision of self. The power of the Great Spirit (as symbolized in the sacred eagle feathers used in ceremonies) transforms Eagle to soar on wings of joy above all limitation. It is the courage of the higher self that speaks of higher truths and constantly reaches towards those heights that others only dare dream of. Call upon Eagle when you need courage to stand up for yourself, speak your truth to others and really walk your talk.

Position

Kneel on the floor, legs bent beneath you, knees slightly apart. Sit so your weight is centred over your heels with your back relaxed and straight. Raise your arms straight out in front of you, with the palms of your hands flat against one another, to form an arrowhead. Move your thumbs so they are folded inside your palms and you can see a small diamond shape of light formed by the gaps between your fingertips. Now, keeping your shoulders down, lift your chin up 5–6 cm (2–3 ins) until your throat feels free. Next slowly move your extended arms to point gently upwards, until you can focus your eyes through one of the diamond shapes. The arms form your eagle's beak, pointing towards the sun.

Breathe your energy up to the throat with the colour blue, then slowly exhale, each time allowing your body to relax into the position a little more. Silently call upon the energy of Eagle to be with you and on the next outbreath begin to sound an *ee*, focusing on the throat. Continue to breathe in cleansing breaths and breathe out *ee*, imagining you are expressing everything you want to say with the sound. Feel it vibrating around your throat, clearing the blocks, releasing the old energy of all those times you kept silent when you should have spoken. Pause for a while in your toning, and experience the silence. Be aware of how your body, your mind and your emotions feel. If you want to scream like Eagle, expressing your highest truth at the top of your voice, do so.

Now continue with the sound and direct it through your 'beak' hands like a laser beam, seeing your truth shooting out into the world and lighting up the skies. Know that when you are filled with spirit you have the courage to say, to do and to be whatever and whosoever you want. Leave your limitations behind and travel with the sound as it strengthens and inspires every single part of you. Continue to tone until you feel this strength and peace in your very being. Find a new freedom with Eagle and communicate the truth of your own spirit to the whole world.

Owl: Wisdom

Sound: ohm
Chakra: third eye
Colour: indigo
Energy: inner seeing

Lyrics:
Wisdom is the gift I bring
I see into your soul
Night and day I know the truth
To live it is my goal
Sing wise owl, sing *ohm*
Sing wise owl, sing *ohm*

Owl Position

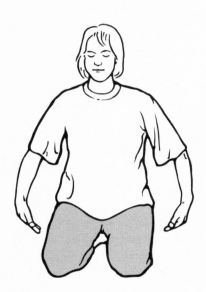

Properties

Owl is an ancient symbol for depicting wisdom. Whether it is night or day, Owl unblinkingly sees the truth and cannot be deceived. Owl's head can turn almost a full circle to follow your movements, while the eyes appear to remain fixed, staring and all-knowing. While most of us are afraid of the dark, 'Night

Eagle' Owl welcomes it. With magical powers of silent observation, Owl sees straight through every situation to uncover the truth, for true wisdom is the ability to perceive what others cannot. Use Owl to help you develop your intuition, delve into the dark secrets in all areas of your life and see the truth.

Position

Kneel on the floor, legs bent beneath you, knees slightly apart. Sit so your weight is centred over your heels, with your back relaxed and straight. Hold your arms slightly out from the side of your body in a gentle curve to represent Owl's wings, fingers curved together and pointing in towards your thighs. Close your eyes and breathe the energy and the colour indigo right the way up to your third eye. Slowly exhale, each time allowing your body to relax into the position a little more.

Silently call upon the energy of Owl to be with you. Breathe in again, and on the outbreath begin to sound an *ohm*, focusing on the brow chakra. Feel your third eye opening and visualize sound and colour pouring through it. Allow the *m* of the *ohm* to vibrate through the bone structure of your face, clearing away all negative energy. Know that there is an inner source of wisdom and knowledge hidden deep within you, an inner voice which will always speak the truth, an inner light which will shine clarity wherever you choose to direct it.

Continue to breathe in cleansing breaths and breathe out *ohm*, sending the light of your intuition to see clearly a person or situation or part of yourself that needs clarity. Pause for a while in your toning, and experience the silence. Be aware of how your body, mind and emotions feel. Use this new wisdom if necessary to heal what you have just seen by calling upon the qualities you've worked with so far – love, understanding, compassion and gentleness. Start the *ohm* again and alternate with periods of silence until you feel clear, calm and peacefully in contact with your inner self.

Spider: Creation

Sound: *ooh*
Chakra: crown
Colour: purple
Energy: universal love

Lyrics:

I weave a web of wonders
On the wheel of life I spin
I choose the golden threads of love
New patterns then begin
Sing spider, sing *ooh*
Sing spider, sing *ooh*

Spider Position

Properties

Spider weaves the Web of Life, intricately beautiful and complex and with eight legs attached to the figure-eight-shaped body symbolizes eternity and represents the female creative energy. If you watch Spider, you will understand that the web each of us spins is nothing less than our own Wheel of Life. We alone are responsible for the complicated patterns we weave and the choices we make. Spider reminds us of our own power as infinitely creative beings to change our lives and mastermind new alternatives. When we spin in service to humanity, using universal love as our thread, we create an everlasting tapestry of joy for the generations to come. Call upon Spider when you want to create something new in your own life or in the world.

Position

Kneel on the floor, legs bent beneath you, knees slightly apart. Sit so your weight is centred over your heels, with your back relaxed and straight, hands resting gently on your knees. Breathe your energy up to the crown with the colour purple and then slowly exhale, each time allowing your body to relax into the position a little more. Breathe in again, silently calling upon the energy of Spider to be with you, and on the outbreath begin to sound an *ooh*, focusing on the crown chakra. Imagine your crown opening, and a shaft of purple light entering from above. Continue to tone and slowly raise your hands until they are directly above your head, reaching to the heavens. See the purple light turning into a purple thread of universal love and begin to weave with it, pulling into your Web of Life everything you want for yourself and the planet. Use every vestige of your imagination to create exciting new pictures and ideas. As you pull the energy in, build your circular web right around yourself from every side right down to the ground, and then up again. You are revitalizing your aura and choosing to use your own creative power to draw positive energy to you. Continue as long as you like.

Pause for a while in your toning, and experience the silence.

Be aware of how your body, mind and emotions feel. Allow the colour purple to flood through you, and feel the peace and contentment of being truly loved and supported. Now commence the *ooh* again, this time using your hands and arms in a circular motion to send the patterns of love and new images out into the world. Continue to tone as long as you like. Your creativity is infinite!

Butterfly: Transformation

Sound: *I am*
           Using the whole body
Colour: white
Energy: creating light body

Lyrics:
I am my own creation
I am ready to take flight
I spread my brightly coloured wings
And fly into the light
Sing butterfly *I am*
Sing butterfly *I am*

Properties

Butterfly flies through the air, carried on the brightly coloured wings of its own individual beauty. The power of the air represents the power of the mind, for we are all a work of art, endlessly re-creating ourselves. From the tiny egg of one idea, nurtured deep within us, the larva of awareness wriggles into life to spin like Spider and create a protective cocoon around itself. Only when we are ready and the warm rays of love penetrate our protection can the chrysalis give birth to a brand-new creation: you!

Are you ready to transform yourself? The preceding seven sound animals have helped you to align yourself to the highest in you. Now ask Butterfly to help you see exactly where you are on the path of your life. Who are you about to become? Enter the chrysalis of your inner self and allow yourself to emerge

Butterfly Position

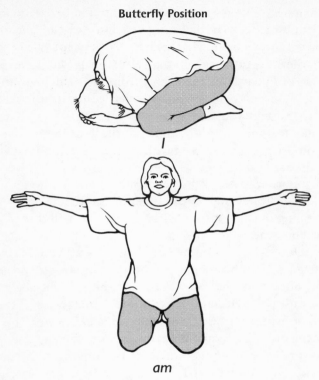

am

experiencing your full beauty. Spread the wings of your own joyful individuality to express the new you.

Position

Kneel on the floor, legs tucked under, feet beneath your seat and knees slightly apart. If you cannot perform this exercise with your knees apart, close them. Place your hands, fingers clasped, on the top of your head, bringing your elbows in to shoulder width. Now very slowly and gently lean forward, allowing your torso to bend between your open knees until your forehead touches the floor, supported on either side by your elbows. Breathe in deeply, imagining you are drawing pure white light into every area of your body.

Slowly exhale, each time allowing yourself to relax into the position a little more. If you find this position uncomfortable, try bringing your knees closer together. Silently call upon the energy of Butterfly to be with you, imagining you are encased in the silence and protection of the chrysalis. Now breathe in again, and on the outbreath begin to sound the words *I am*, calling into every part of your body the energy from the earth beneath you and the air around you. What is it that you want to be born? Who is the real you and what are your gifts to the world? Continue to tone, clearly holding an image of the new you in your mind and empowering it with the sound. Pause for a while, and experience the silence. Be aware of how your body, mind and emotions feel. Allow the new vision of yourself to flow into every cell of your body as you breathe. See the nuclei of your cells beating in harmony and strength to affirm all that you are and will become.

Begin to sing *I am*. On the *I* gradually uncurl your body and head to an upright position, allowing your arms to extend either side of you so that by the *am* they stretch out at right-angles like wings, with palms facing forwards. Hold the posture, feel the energy of expressing who you are, curl back down again and repeat the process as many times as you like.

If you are supple enough this can be done from a standing position, with head tucked into slightly bent knees and the whole body gradually straightening upwards to the arms-extended position with the words *I am*.

By the end of Butterfly, if you have worked your way through the eight Medicine Sound Animals you should have experienced a transformation. Now all you have to do is spread your beautiful coloured wings and fly joyfully into the light.

Animal Messengers

You can use the Sound Animals as much as you like, working with them individually, two or three at a time, or the whole group one after another. One word of warning, when you start working in this way, the real animals may begin to appear in your life. If this happens, take time to tune into the animal and ask what message it has to bring you.

In our highly sophisticated and increasingly industrialized

society we have the mistaken conception that the earth belongs to us. We have forgotten that we share the planet with every created living thing, and as we claim more and more land for ourselves there is less and less room for the animals. When an animal comes to share your home or garden, try not to kill it. It has as much right to be there as you have. If you are arachnophobic, ask someone to capture your spider invader in a glass and put it outside. Or you can simply ask animals and insects to leave, as I have often done with armies of ants and marauding wasps. Once you understand that animals are bringing you messages, an exciting new world opens up.

Healing Animals with Sound

Animals respond well to healing as they are highly sensitive to energies. You can communicate with any animal by using any of the tones we've already worked with. Treat the healing session in exactly the same way as you would for a human being. Use your intuition to find out where and what sound the animal needs, empower your voice with the energy and use gentle, soothing tones. Like us, they shut off and become aggressive when rejected and hurt, and respond best to tenderness and loving care.

SOUND ANIMALS SONG

Music and lyrics: © The Singing Earth Music Company Ltd.
Shirlie Roden   London 1998

Chapter 9

HEALING THE EARTH WITH SOUND

The earth is not sick. It's the people. If you really want to learn about love, take a look at Mother Earth. She gives us everything we need to live – house materials, food, even the clothing we wear. We have a natural Indian law that you must give something back to the earth before you can take, and you must never abuse the earth, because it's a living entity. We're only a part of it.

Tim Sikyea, Medicine Man, Dog Rib Tribe

When Angelica Roquas Hammer channelled her reading for me on sound healing, I was allowed to take in some questions from a friend of mine, an international actor, with regard to how we could work together with sound and music to energize the large audience already at his disposal. Neither of us expected the answer which came back which revealed yet another dimension of healing with sound. We were told to go to sacred sites, power points and caves and use our voices to chant, sing and tone, sending circular waves of sound into the earth which would create healing vibrations. If enough people did this, balance could be maintained with the seas, the earth, the land and the weather, and life would be enhanced, for the sound would actually help the trees to grow.

It had never occurred to me that in the same way as pure vibrations release and heal a human being, so could they cleanse, purify and energize the planet, but it wasn't long before life presented me with someone who was actually doing just that. Beautiful Painted Arrow (Joseph Rael) was a shaman of the Pueblo Indian tradition. In a state of meditation, he had received a vision. He was surrounded by angels who had placed a baby on the earth in front of him. As a circle of light spread around the child, he saw that it was to be a circular chamber for transmitting sound. When I met Joseph, he was travelling the world, building his underground 'sound chambers' to be used for prayer, meditation and chanting with the specific focus of sending the sound into the earth for healing.

I never experienced Joseph's sound chambers, but some years later, I found myself in a vast network of Slovenian underground lakes and caves called Križna Jama with a friend. It was off-season so we had the entire place to ourselves. We clambered for hours over rocky pathways, past ancient bear bones, crossing icy lagoons in a rubber dinghy. Deep in the heart of the caves, we stopped in the middle of a small lake and turned off our lamps. The darkness was profound. I could not see my hand in front of my face. I made a prayer for the earth, called the Angels of Sound to be with me, and began to issue tones – long, pure, high notes which echoed through the silence and filtered off into distant passages. With each note I sent out love and compassion, then listened as it reverberated into the distance. I continued for some time until it seemed as though the entire cave structure was filled with the vibration of my voice. Then I stopped, and we sat in complete silence. Suddenly I heard laughter. It seemed to come from the very walls of the caves themselves – light, silvery whispers. My logical mind said I was imagining it. We were miles from anywhere, deep underground, and no one else was in the caves that day. Mesmerized, I sat listening to the ghostly whispering until it became too much for me. I switched my lamp on and the spell was broken. There was my friend, the boat, the freezing water. Nothing more. Hours later when we were driving home, I hestitantly shared my experience and was astounded when my friend admitted he'd heard the whispering voices too. We could find no logical explanation but instinctively I felt it was to do with the sounds I had sent out. Something, on some level, had responded.

There is a wonderful Slovenian called Marko Pogačnik who uses lithopuncture for healing (a similar principle to acupuncture in humans), placing stones as 'needles' in energetic points in the earth. For many years he has seen what he calls 'the intelligence of nature' or the elemental earth beings in their physical form and even talked to them. As mankind haphazardly destroys vegetation and power points on the earth, many elementals are displaced, together with the earth's natural harmony and balance. Part of Marko's work is to re-create safe spaces for the elementals to inhabit, as they are vital to the earth's energy. I believe I made contact with the elementals that day with my sound; and my continuing aim now is to do all I can to help realign, regenerate and revive the earth.

Cellular Memory of the Earth

I was once asked to lead a group to various sites in a village which the locals felt needed healing. Making sacred sound, we started with a church on top of a hill where centuries before women had been burned as witches and some hours later arrived at our final destination: a wooded dell by the side of a country lane. As I made the closing prayers to focus our energies on the earth, the unlikely words spilled from my mouth requesting healing also 'for anyone who had been raped and murdered'.

It was only afterwards they told me a young girl had in fact been raped and murdered on that very spot. Like us, the earth holds memories in her cellular structure, and the most compassionate thing we can do is to help her release the violence and abuse trapped in her 'skin'. When we heal the earth, it connects us to what needs to be healed in ourselves; and conversely, when we heal ourselves, we also gain greater understanding as to how and where the earth most needs help.

Sing to Nature

My 'acupuncture Indians' had told me to sing for the pure joy of singing, and it was only after I actually began to do this that I realized how deeply-ingrained was my belief that I should only sing when I got paid. As I began to use my talents in service, a completely different area opened up. Then I sang to nature, and an amazing thing happened. I became one with it.

Singing and chanting in the great outdoors is such a powerful focus. Nowadays there are Rainbow Gatherings and indigenous music festivals where you can experience the 'unplugged' pleasures of drumming and chanting on the earth. So go back to your roots and call upon your ancestors. Stand firm and strong on the soil, and sing to nature: to the plants, the trees and flowers, the water and the wind, the insects and the animals, the rocks, the sun and the moon. Chant, make tones, sing your favourite song – but sing for pure joy, out in the open, under the sky, no matter what the weather, the time of day or year. You will be surprised at what happens.

Working with the Elements

Although it is generally agreed there are four elements – earth, water, air and fire – they are not all elements in the true sense of the word – that is, single entities. For instance, earth is a mixture, and air contains many gases including oxygen and nitrogen. The ancient meaning of the four elements relates to them being the basics of life. Thus I have added wood, stone and metal to the list for purifying with sound, using the word 'element' in a more general sense.

You can work with each element individually, day by day, or you can move from one to the next in a single session, and although you can perform all these rituals alone, the more people you can get to form a circle, the more powerful the effect will be. So far I have only worked with groups above ground, but if you decide to go down into caves, *please* make sure they are safe and there is no danger of accidents.

Choose very carefully where you want to work. There are obvious power points on the earth's surface – many churches, ancient monuments and stone circles are built on them – and there are corresponding ley lines often harking back to prehistoric tracks which join these prominent points. However, sometimes these places lack privacy. A good way to locate a power point is to look for an unusual natural physical feature, such as an odd crop of trees or formation of stones. You can also pendulum the earth, use divining rods or rely upon your intuition, allowing yourself to be drawn to a particular place. Trust the energy that pulls you there and know that wherever you choose, however unlikely it may seem, it will surely be the right place.

In the sections that follow, I am not going to give you a particular vowel sound to work with. It is up to you to tune into your site, the weather and the energy of the participants to decide what feels appropriate. By now, you should be adept at using tones and you will soon be aware of anything that does not work. I also like to use my Indian drum or sometimes a rain stick, Tibetan cymbals, or a bell. Didgeridoos, gongs and conch shells work well outside too.

First, ask everybody to stand in a circle, barefoot if possible so people can really feel the ground beneath them. Before I begin any ceremonies, I like to make a prayer offering of thanks to the earth. This can be done in whatever tradition you are most comfortable with. The Native Americans use tobacco, but you can bring favourite food, flowers or whatever is available (so long as it's biodegradable). The Peruvian Incas have a wonderful ceremony called Pacha Mama where they make stunningly beautiful designs on the earth from flowers and food. So make your prayers as you wish and offer your gift to the Earth Mother.

Next, I like to tune everyone in to the heart energy of the group. Ask everyone to turn sideways with the left shoulder pointing to the centre of the circle, raise both hands with palms facing towards the back of the heart centre of the person in front and, using the sound *oh* and visualizing the colour green, send the energy and sound in through the back of that person's heart and out through the front, so that it moves around the circle. Continue for as long as you like until the sound feels free, clear and strong. Now you're ready to begin.

Earth

Everyone in the circle now faces inwards again, eyes closed, hands at their sides, knees slightly bent, feet shoulder-width apart. Guide them to focus on their breathing, the beating of their hearts, the aliveness of the earth and their connection to the trees, the rocks, the animals and each other. Now ask them to imagine they have strong, vibrant red roots growing into the earth from the soles of their feet. See the layers of rock, clay and water as the roots grow down, deeper and deeper, until they almost reach the centre of the earth. Allow time to really feel the richness of the earth and the solidity of being rooted in it.

Choosing a sound, begin to emit tones and ask the group to stretch out their hands, palms facing downwards to tune in to the pain of the earth. As they make the sound, they can bend closer to the ground until their hands almost touch it. Focus on those places which have been destroyed, violated and polluted by violence, wars, mass destruction, hatred, massacres, ethnic cleansings, rapes and murders.

You are now going to draw all this from the earth. Slowly come to an upright position again. With eyes open, point the hands down towards the earth at forty-five degrees, using the sound to lift the negative energy. Continue with the sound, and move the hands upwards until you are pointing directly into the sky. Envisage that you are literally sucking the negativity out of the earth and channelling it into the heavens. Continue with the group in this way, working rhythmically together until the area feels cleansed.

Close the eyes again, hands by the side, relax, and concentrate on breathing for a few minutes.

Now reverse the process, this time using the sound to pull down positive energy from the sky and channel it into the earth. Point the hands skywards and imagine you are an electricity conductor. Feel the energy literally running into your hands and arms, and as you emit the sound, slowly lower the hands until they are pointing directly into the earth again. Feel the healing energy pouring from your fingertips. Continue to focus the positive energy down in this way until the area feels strong and vibrant and healed.

End the process by standing once more with eyes closed, focusing on your roots in the earth. Feel its richness, nourishment and vitality travelling up the roots into your central nervous system, filling you with vibrancy. Slowly pull the roots up again into the body, open your eyes, and bless the earth.

Water

Water symbolizes the emotions. What can be more healing, revitalizing and relaxing than pure, crystal clear water – either to drink, swim in or bathe and shower. Yet how carelessly we treat it, thoughtlessly polluting it in a million different ways. Toxic chemicals, high levels of the female hormone oestrogen and other pollution go into the water system and enter the food chain where they not only damage and destroy our health, but that of innocent creatures and plants which need it to survive. Who would ever have thought we would have to bottle our water to be sure it was safe enough to drink?

To work with water, first bring some with you in a container. Offer it to the heavens with a prayer of thanks and then pour it on the earth. Tune your circle of people in by sending sound through the hearts as previously described, and follow with the meditation to root into the earth, this time sending the roots below the rock and clay layers until they reach the subterranean lakes.

Begin to emit the chosen tone, asking the group to stretch out their hands, palms facing downwards, to tune into the polluted water element in the earth. Again, bend slowly down until the hands almost touch the ground, focusing on chemical and industrial pollution, sewerage, detergent, household cleaners, floating garbage, oil slicks, acid rain. Feel the sadness of the water, the floods and the rivers bursting their banks with the imbalance man has created.

You are now going to become a pump. Slowly return to upright, open your eyes and turn with your left shoulder facing in and left hand pointing down, right arm stretched upwards towards the sky. Using your chosen sound, pump the pollution from the earth through your left hand into the right arm and out of the fingers, channelling it into the sky. Continue until the water in that area feels clear and refreshed. Close your eyes again, hands by the side, relax and concentrate on breathing for a few minutes.

Now reverse the process so the right shoulder faces inwards

with right hand pointing downwards, left arm reaching up to the sky. Focus the group on pure rainwater, clear, refreshing and energizing. Use sound to call that healing energy down the left arm, into the right arm and into the earth, envisaging this pure water filling the lakes, streams, rivers and subterranean reservoirs. Continue until the water in that area feels refreshed and revitalized.

End the process by standing once more with eyes closed. Focus on your roots, as they reach deep down into the underground lakes. Feel the richness, nourishment and vitality of the water travelling up the roots into your body, cleansing and purifying you. Slowly pull your roots up again into the body, open your eyes and bless the water.

Air

While researching for a Welsh musical recently, I read some nineteenth-century descriptions of the South Wales valleys. The most surprising thing was how all those valleys were once covered with trees where nightingales sang and the sweetness of the wild flowers floated on the air. There are parts of Europe where mountain and meadow are still decked in variegated colourful blooms which scent the breeze, but the main thing we've managed to add to the air this century is large doses of toxic gases and poisonous emissions.

To work with the air element, begin the process as usual with your ritual prayer and offering. Call the energy of the north, south, west and east winds to be with you. Follow with the heart centre attunement of the group and the meditation to root everybody into the earth.

Now focus the group on breathing in through the nose, down the imaginery 'channel of air' to the sacral chakra, releasing the breath with your chosen sound. As they gently continue this process, ask them to tune into the pollution in the air: toxic chemical emissions from factories, cars, chimneys, rubbish tips, sprays, fertilizers, fires and CFCs (chlorofluorocarbons).

Firstly, you are going to cleanse the earth. Continuing the tone, ask the group to stretch out their hands, palms facing downwards, to tune into the poisonous gases man has created in the earth. Bend slowly until the hands almost touch the ground, and as you come up again, use the sound to pull the gases out of the earth with the hands, ending by stretching them above the head to release into the atmosphere. Continue this process until you feel the surrounding earth is clear.

Now you are going to work with the air itself, acting as a transformer as you visualize pulling the pollution from the atmosphere down through your energy centres to be cleansed. Place the hands above the head, palms together. As you emit sound, draw the hands slowly down to the crown chakra. When you reach the level of the crown, take the right hand out to the right and the left hand to the left in a circular movement, describing a circle in the air above until the palms join together again. Repeat three times, and on the last time, as you describe the circle, end with hands reaching up to the sky.

Repeat the process by placing the hands above the head again, palms together, this time drawing them down to the third eye chakra, then do the same for throat, heart, solar plexus, sacral and root until you have cleared the air through your whole body. Close the eyes, hands by the side, relax and concentrate on breathing for a few minutes. Now repeat the process once more, but this time use the sound to pull down clear, unpolluted air from the highest planes through your energy centres and out into the surrounding atmosphere. Continue until the surrounding area feels clean and revitalized.

End by standing once more with eyes closed, focusing on your breath as you inhale. Feel the clarity, vitality and tranquillity of pure air as you breathe it into your whole body, sending it down through your roots into the earth. Slowly pull the roots up again into the body, open your eyes and bless the air.

Fire

Start by lighting a candle and make a prayer to the fire element. Offer the candle to the heavens and place it on the earth. Next, tune the group in to the heart energy, followed by the meditation to root them into the earth.

Now begin to emit the chosen tone, asking the group to stretch out their hands, palms facing downwards, to tune into the heat of the earth, bending down until the hands almost touch the ground. Ask them to focus on the heat caused by nuclear bombs, landmines and explosions, industrial factories, machinery, burning gases and fossil fuels, pollution, forest and bush fires, the harmful rays of the sun unfiltered by the ozone layer. See the parched desert where no life can survive. Continuing with the sound, slowly return to an upright position. Point hands diagonally at the earth and gradually draw the heat upwards from the earth into the sky, until hands and arms are pointing heavenwards. Continue until the surrounding earth feels calm and clear. Close the eyes, hands by the sides, relax and concentrate on breathing for a few minutes.

Now imagine above the group is a huge hole in the ozone layer. See it clearly as a reality. You are now going to use sound to heal and close that hole. Open the eyes, point the hands and arms diagonally above the head into the sky. Lead the group with your chosen sound and envisage the healing energy pouring from your fingertips into the sky. Use the heart energy of the group to fill the hole with healing energy. Continue with the sound until you feel it is completely closed.

Next you are going to pull down the balanced, filtered rays of the sun that are essential to generate life on earth. Pointing hands and arms once more into the sky, emit the chosen tone and slowly lower your stretched-out arms until they point diagonally into the earth, visualizing yourself drawing down the sun's power to heal and revitalize. Continue until the earth feels gently warmed and nourished. End by standing once more with eyes closed, focusing on your roots in the earth. Feel the warmth of the natural life force flowing through you, the sun on your skin and the life-giving force of the golden rays gently filtering down on to the planet. Slowly pull the roots up again into the body, open your eyes and bless the sun.

Wood

I have always felt the calmness and nurturing power of trees. My 'acupuncture Indians' told me to hug them in times when I missed that warm, masculine energy in my life. I have often stood with both arms around a solid trunk, eyes closed, breathing in the strength and eternal nature of a friendly tree. And yes, trees do talk. If you want an answer to a question, just sit with your back against the tree trunk. Go into a meditative state, ask the tree, and the solution will come.

On a recent trip to the Aura-Soma factory in Tetford, Lincolnshire, I visited the Memorial Garden dedicated to founder Vicky Wall. I sat beneath the tree where Vicky had received the colour healing balancing system, and began to meditate. Strange though it may sound, as soon as I sat down, the tree proceeded to tell me that there is an octave in pure sound between each chakra centre (that is, not an octave as the human ear hears it, but on a higher plane of sensitivity), and that each vertebra in the backbone has a musical note corresponding to it. The tree then advised me that to work with really pure sound, I had to be as clear as possible on all levels, and therefore I should not drink *any* alcohol! As I sat in the leafy silence, I understood why we use phrases such as the Tree of Life and the Tree of Knowledge, because not only do trees possess an inherent wisdom, but they love more than anything to share it! A tree is pure living love. They service our lives with wood and paper for every imaginable object, and whatever we do to them – pollute, chop, uproot and burn them – those green shoots reappear in the spring, and they bloom again. So to really understand what it's like to suffer as a tree, we are going to become one.

Make your ritual prayer and offering, and tune in the heart energy of the group as usual. Now ask everyone in the circle to face inwards to the centre, eyes closed, hands at their sides, knees slightly bent, feet shoulder-width apart. Guide them to focus on their breathing, the beating of their hearts, and ask them to imagine they are turning into a tree. Feel the straightness and solidity of the trunk with roots growing deep into the earth, and imagine branches and leaves reaching out towards the sky. Visualize breathing in through the leaves. Feel what it's like to be totally rooted in one place drawing all your nourishment up from the earth through your root system. Now begin to emit your chosen sound and ask people to extend their arms outwards and upwards like branches. Tune in to the pain of the trees that are cut down, burned alive, polluted. With arms outstretched, feel the crucifixion of rainforest, city park, countryside, anywhere where living trees are destroyed and denied the right to live. Experience the leaves inhaling chemical emissions and pollution deep into the body of the tree. Feel the desolation of the scorched earth, the charred forests, the desert lands once canopied with trees. Then use sound to release all that pain through the fingertips into the sky for as long as people can hold their arms up. Allow the arms to drop to the sides to rest. Close the eyes again, relax, and concentrate on breathing for a few minutes.

Open your eyes, continue the sound and raise the arms once more into the tree position. Ask the group to experience their own individual strength as the tree they now are: the solidity of the wood, the depth of the roots holding them firm and drawing up rich nourishment, the fecundity of fruit and seed and leaf-bearing branches, the pride of standing centred and alone. Continue with the sound, and lead the group to truly understand the immensity of what trees give us, from every part of their sacred wood and leaves to the pure clear air they exhale into the atmosphere. Breathe in, as you do so pulling energy up from the roots into your 'branches'. Exhale with your chosen sound and simultaneously send out love. Use the positive tree energy to transform both yourself and any surrounding trees. Really experience what it means to take in the negative, digest it and transmute it to the positive. Continue until you feel the trees in the area have received healing energy back equal to that which they have been sending out for so long. Once you experience in every cell of your body what a tree endlessly gives with its life force, you will never knowingly harm another 'standing person' in your life.

End the process by standing once more with eyes closed,

focusing on your life-giving branches and your roots in the earth. Feel the beauty, strength and power, the endless cycle of rebirth, the nurturing love of the trees. Slowly pull your roots up again into the body, open your eyes and bless the trees.

Stone

When I'm really in tune with myself and everything on the planet, I see the faces in the rocks and stones. There are always crooked smiles grinning up from the boulders and I remember once when I was making sound with an ancient waterfall, how faces appeared in the cliffs, like guardian spirits. In the native Indian Sweat Lodge when the heated rocks are ceremonially brought in ready to transform the water into steam, it's always comforting to see rocky eyes, mouths and noses peering out in the dark, as though the stones were saying, 'Don't worry. We're your friends. We're only here to help your process.'

Crystals are not stones, but we tend to think of them in that way because they're solid. In fact, they're just a different molecular structure of a substance in crystalline physical form. As many are found within the rock structure, I'm going to include them here, so if you have a favourite crystal you want to work with, bring it with you. Or you can tune a set of crystals into the notes of the octave (see Chapter 5), place them in a circle with your chosen stones, and work inside the energy ring.

To work with stone, either find a group of stones or an outcrop you are drawn to. If it's small, form a circle around it. If it's big, work inside. Alternatively, find a 'power point' on the earth and bring some stones that really resonate with you. Make your prayers and offerings to the outcrop, or if you are using your own stones, offer one to the sky and then replace it on the earth. Next, tune the group into the heart energy with sound, followed by the meditation to root them into the earth.

Begin to emit your chosen sound and ask the group to stretch their hands towards the stones to tune into their pain. Focus on those places which have been destroyed and mutilated by man, as we mine for minerals, fossil fuels and precious stones, carve out quarries and gravel pits, excavate motorways and buildings, create landslides and erosion with our lifestyles, and blast out craters and increase the risk of earthquakes with our nuclear weapons of mass destruction.

Continue with the sound and ask the group to raise their arms directly above their heads, pointing vertically into the sky. As they stand in this position, let them envisage themselves becoming ancient standing stones, weathered by thousands of years on the earth. Now lower the arms, pointing them towards the stones again, and use the sound to draw all the negativity from the 'stone people', raising the arms slowly upwards to channel it into the sky. Continue until you feel the stone outcrop or the land in that area is cleansed. Allow the hands to rest by the sides, close the eyes again, relax, and concentrate on breathing for a few minutes.

Now reverse the process, this time using the sound to pull down positive energy from the sky and channel it into the stones. Point the hands skywards and imagine you are part of an ancient stone pyramid. Feel the energy running into your hands, arms and body like an electric shock, and as you emit the sound, slowly lower the hands until they are pointing directly at the stones. Feel the power of prehistoric monuments, rocky plateaux and high peaks, volcanic rocks and mountain ranges pouring from your fingertips. Invoke the positive energy of crystalline structures, quartz mountains, stalagmites and stalagtites. See the stones come alive, transformed into shining crystal pillars that receive and transmit pure light and sound. Continue to focus the sound in this way until the stones and surrounding area feel strong, vibrant and healed.

End the process by standing once more with eyes closed, focusing on your roots and your solidity as you stand upon the earth. Feel the eternal wisdom, the timelessness of these ancient 'stone people'. Experience their strength, power and calmness, their stillness. Know the deep peace of being buffeted by the storms of life and surviving, weathered, yet unchanged. We *are* liquid crystalline structures ourselves. Allow yourself to feel that pure clear energy flowing within you. Slowly pull your roots up from the earth into the body again, open eyes, and bless the stones and crystals.

Metal

Metals are a class of elements that are typically lustrous solids (mercury being an exception, as it is normally liquid) and have particular properties such as being good conductors of heat and electricity. Different metals and other elements are sometimes mixed together to create metal alloys (pewter, for instance, is an alloy of tin and lead). For the purposes of sound healing, please be aware that when I use the terms 'metal', it is generalized to include gold, silver, copper, zinc, tin, iron, steel, nickel, lead, foil and mesh and so on.

Make your offering to the earth as usual, tune your circle of people in by sending sound through their hearts and follow with the meditation to root them into the earth. Choose your sound and begin to emit tones, asking the group to stretch out their hands, palms facing downwards to tune in to the pain of the earth. We are going to focus on discarded human *junk*: rubbish dumps and land fills with non-biodegradable metallic waste, nuclear waste, poisonous metals (like lead pipes), old car tips, abandoned oil rigs, sunken wrecks and ships, motorway and plane crashes, buried land mines, unexploded bombs, shrapnel and bullet cases, mesh, barbed wire, old steel girders and anything we have thoughtlessly abandoned.

As the group makes the chosen sound, ask them to bend closer to the ground until their hands almost touch it, feeling the negative vibration of all our polluting metal junk. They are now going to become alchemists, transforming base metal into gold, only instead of the ancient 'philosopher's gold', they are going to use sound. Slowly bring them to an upright position again. With eyes closed, ask everyone to point their hands to the centre of the circle, arms at shoulder height. Use the sound to create a 'melting pot' and visualize all the junk being sucked into the centre of the circle. Continue the sound until you feel everything has been melted down into liquid metal. Rest your hands by your sides, relax, and concentrate on breathing for a few minutes.

Now open your eyes, point your hands towards the heavens and use sound to pull the positive energy from the sky into the centre of the pool, slowly lowering hands and arms as you do so. Energize the molten metal until it becomes a golden nourishing pool of liquid energy. See it seeping slowly into the earth, a healing, soothing elixir.

End the process by standing once more with eyes closed, focusing on your roots in the earth. Feel this golden vitality travelling up your roots into your central nervous system, filling every cell of your body and spilling out into your aura, so that as true alchemy takes place within your shadow self, you begin to emanate pure golden light. Slowly pull the roots up again into the body, open your eyes and bless the metals.

Sound, Movement and the Elements for Self-Healing

Although I have described a fairly stationary process for working with these elements for earth healing, they can also be used for group and self-healing in conjunction with sound and movement. All you need to do is ask your group to focus on one element at a time and 'become' it, while simultaneously making whatever continuous sound and movement that intuitively comes to them. Lead them through the process with a guided meditation of words suggesting the properties of the element. It is important that they keep moving and making the sound, so encourage them to do so as you speak.

The American Indians say 'Walk like a living prayer, your feet resting on the earth, your spirit reaching way up into the sky, your body linking the sacred beneath with the sacred above.' Only then can we experience the Sacred Hoop of Oneness – a union of earth, sky and all living things. Your sound is needed. Ask for the highest in yourself to link in pure tones with the highest vibrations of sound and light, and our planet will be a better place for your voice adding harmony and balance to the earth.

EPILOGUE: ONE LAST WORD FROM THE ANGELS OF SOUND

We have now travelled worlds and dimensions together on our mutual journey of discovery. As I have stressed throughout these pages, make your prayers and attunements, offer yourself in service, and follow your intuition. Once you begin to work with the Angels of Sound you will develop your own rituals and practices, and each time they will give you something new so that it is a continuous process of creativity and healing, for the Angels of Sound are very special teachers who rarely touch the earth plane. Listen carefully and you will hear their laughter, for they have a great sense of humour. 'If you could hear sometimes with your ears on these planes what a discord mankind can create, the sound they issue forth unknowing,' they told me in a channelled reading, 'it is an *absolute din*!'

I have to agree with them. So as we purify with sound and hold sacred ourselves and the planet, as we think, act, live and relate in harmony to every created living thing, our total vibration will rise like a prayer of sound and light into the heavens and our souls will add their notes of beauty to the symphony of the universe. Know how powerful you are in this, and know how joyful is the pure music of your singing spirit. It's as simple and as magnificent as that.

USEFUL ADDRESSES

The Sound, Colour and Movement Exercises plus Medicine Sound Animal songs and a guided sound meditation are available on Shirlie Roden's *Sound Healing* CD from:
QED, Lancaster Road, New Barnet, Hertfordshire, EN4 8AS. Tel: 0181 441 7722 or see their website www.qedproductions.com/retail.htm
Also available from QED is the sound and music transformational double CD *Free the Butterfly*, by Suzi Quatro and Shirlie Roden.

For further information on Aura-Soma products contact:
Aura-Soma, South Road, Tetford, Horncastle, Lincolnshire, LN9 6QB. Tel: 01507 533581 or see their website www.aura-soma.co.uk
Or contact their shop Lucia Angelis, 69a Endell Street, Covent Garden, London, WC2H 9AJ. Tel: 0171 240 6226.

Paul Solomon died in 1994 leaving behind a legacy of tapes with his Fellowship of the Inner Light. For further information contact:
The Fellowship of the Inner Light, 620 14th Street, Virginia Beach 23451, USA. Tel: (757) 426 5782. For a copy of their UK catalogue send £2.00 (cheques made payable to F.I.L. in the UK, which is refunded when you order your first tape) to F.I.L. in the UK, PO Box 23, Sandhurst, Berkshire, GU47 9XX.

For further information on the F.I.L. Annual Family Gathering in Slovenia:
Breda Vukelj, Kajuhova 11, 4260 Bled, Slovenia. Tel: (386) 64 745880 or e-mail: aval@perftech.si

Dr David Schweitzer's research on sound therapy can be located on the internet at http://www.davidschweitzer.com

FURTHER READING

J. W. Armstrong, *Water of Life*, Health Science Press (1971) – on urine therapy.

Peter Kelder, *Tibetan Secrets of Youth and Vitality*, Thorsons (1988) – on Tibetan exercises.

Wa-Na-Nee-Che with Eliana Harvey, *White Eagle Medicine Wheel – Native American Wisdom as a Way of Life*, Connections Book Publishing (1977) – on medicine animals.

Jamie Sams and David Carson, *Medicine Cards – The Discovery of Power Through the Ways of Animals*, Bear and Company (1988) – also on medicine animals.

Joseph Rael/Beautiful Painted Arrow, *Being and Vibration*, Council Oak Books (1992) – sound chambers.

INDEX